Dedicated to my parents Reginald E. McKamie Sr, Geneva Winfield,
my partner Simeilia Hodge-Dallaway
and
to all the Unheard Voices… we will tell your stories.

First published in 2017 by Oberon Books Ltd
521 Caledonian Road, London N7 9RH
Tel: +44 (0) 20 7607 3637 / Fax: +44 (0) 20 7607 3629
e-mail: info@oberonbooks.com
www.oberonbooks.com

A catalogue record for this book is available from the British Library.

PB ISBN: 9781786821515
E ISBN: 9781786821522

Cover image by Black Lives, Black Words

Designed by Konstantinos Vasdekis

Printed and bound by 4edge Limited, Essex, UK.
eBook conversion by Lapiz Digital Services, India.

Visit www.oberonbooks.com to read more about all our books and to buy them. You will also find features, author interviews and news of any author events, and you can sign up for e-newsletters so that you're always first to hear about our new releases.

CONTENTS

Introduction

It's on us. It's always been on us.

From Claudia Jones to Michael X, from Frank Crichlow to Darcus Howe to Doreen and Neville Lawrence, there is a rich and fierce tradition of resistance that has defined the past century in this great city.

2016 was a significant year in the UK. Following the Brexit vote to take us out of the European Union, few of us could have predicted the steep rise in racially motivated hate crime, or the vitriol that was unleashed on the 'immigrant', a term which became a dangerous and charged catch-all and scapegoat. And a term that, in the eyes of the dominant right-wing media, is almost always defined as non-white. That exists outside the bubble of privilege and power occupied by wealthy, white Europeans.

It has been twelve months in which our world seems to have shrunk around us, to have become smaller and more insular. Many of us who had always called this country home, suddenly began to question what home really meant.

Eight years ago, when the first presidency of an African American was in its infancy, many looked forward to a new horizon, to a post-racial reality. Instead, the list of Black lives violently ended, of justice miscarried, has only grown longer and more terrible. Against this backdrop, we've seen a rise of right-wing thought in both volume and acceptability, from the anti-Islamic, anti-immigrant rhetoric of a new breed of populist politician through the proliferation of the Alt-Right, to the very different president now squatting in the White House.

Black Lives Matters is different in both form and function from the civil rights movements of the past. As Jeff Chang notes in his extraordinary book *We Gon' Be Alright*, this was not a movement which formed around one forceful, charismatic male voice. It was started by three women: Alicia Garza, Patrisse Cullors and Opal Tometi. It is an insurgent movement; a reaction; a disruption. It has a sense of urgency, of crisis and of place. It represents the latest form in a continuum of struggle that stretches back as far as slavery, a new, horizontal, open source resistance.

It speaks to an American reality, a 21st century reality, to the prison-industrial complex, urban poverty, and the frustration of an underclass who found themselves left in limbo and threatened by systemic violence even under Obama.

I have been struck by how the media perception of the Black Lives Matter movement has seen it framed as a negative force

A twelve-year-old kid stands behind a box of bootleg DVDS and CDs. His name is Lil' J.

Say man…say man…say hold up hold up, playa… I got that hotness right here three for ten. What you looking for? I got them all man. DVDs, CDs what you lookin' for? What you lookin' for? Cause I got it right here at Lil' J's Discount Bootleg! Oh…aight…aight I feel you… Take care of your self man. You take care of your self. It's cool thank you for not supporting your neighborhood entre-po-negro…huh? Oh, it's cool… I got honorary status.

Lil' J takes a joint out of his back pocket and about to smoke.

What you mean I can't smoke? I'm stressin' man… I'm fuckin' stressin'over here. It sucks not having Big E out here with me. Now he could hustle. That man was a hustler for real. True King of the Chi-town Hustle!!!

Silence.

I miss my brotha. Anyway I got problems man, you feel me… mo money, mo problems… Hell more like the less money in your pocket the mo problems you got…

Lil' J puts the joint away and notices that a possible customer is walking by.

Hey player…hey player… I got some hot DVDs for sale anything you want I got it…What you looking for…Bastard. Anyway where was I… Oh yeah. Where was Big E…Big E was the man. Not scared of nothing. Man, onetime this cop comes approaching us about sellin' when we were in front of a Blockbuster. Guess they didn't like us taking their business from them and the cop is like "You can't be solicitin' your shit over here." Big E looked at the cop and said "We ain't solicitin' shit, We Entre-po-negroes, we're selling shit get your mind right policeman." That shit cracked me up…even though we can never go around that Blockbuster anymore.

Pause.

Yeah, I'm going to visit him, it's always good to see E. Big E's my hero man. So if you interested in buying some DVDs man, that would help me out a lot… I'd be able to go visit Big E… Haven't seen him in awhile. I want to surprise him I think he'd be happy to see me. But I got to get enough to make three or four good bus transfers to get to him. I don't know… Big E always knew how to get everywhere. I ain't never been good about that shit… I just follow Big E, you know. Everybody respected Big E. I mean everybody.

One time this guy comes up to me. Big brollic lookin' no neck havin' muthaphucka…anyway he rolls up on me mad cause I'm selling bootlegs on his block and he has me up against the wall you know about to beat me down bad and Big E gets there and saves me you know. He's like "Hey man, let little man do what he do, he's not hurting you. You sell weed, he sells movies. We all got what the other wants... Let's keep shit kosher cause eventually you going to want to buy a movie and I know we eventually going to want to buy some weed. So chill man...chill man. Can't we all get along."

Pause.

Yeah, man... Big E is my hero, man... I'm trying to go see him. He always made me feel safe, never had a family before not really. Big E is the closest thing I've ever had to a big brotha.

Pause.

Sometimes it would get late and it would be too late for me to get home by myself cause that's how you get fucked up around here rollin' by yourself with merchandise you know and he'd let me stay at his place. It's a small room in this crack hotel, you know with free porn on the tv and no heat over on that Chinatown Red... but it's his home and so I'd sleep there. But I at least know I'm safe with him there and sometime it would get cold you know and I'd be on the floor like usual sleeping... shivering cause it's cold but trying to sleep. And Big E, he'd say "Hey punk ass. Come here." And he'd let me crawl into bed with him and he'd hold me, hold me in his big arms. And he'd tell me. "I love you little bro." And I'd know I'm going to be alright...I know I'm going to be safe...That nothing could hurt me cause I know he was going to look out for me whether it was on a cold night in a shitty hotel or out on these streets. I knew he was going to be there for me.

Last night I slept at his place without him. I didn't feel so safe you know. All because I didn't listen to Big E. He told me don't go nowhere alone with merchandise and these cops pulled up and started messin' with me. Tossing me back and forth and thinking they're teaching me a lesson and shit and everybody respected Big E. So you know, He comes up to them to stop them and they're telling to back the hell up and show some ID... and he reaches into his back pocket to get his ID... and... That's all he was doing just reaching into his back pocket for his ID and then... and then...You people claiming... and when I mean people I mean the cops... said he had a weapon, claiming he was this huge monster that they felt their lives were endangered, media paints him as the worse man walkin', but shit just ask the people that knew him... just ask the people that knew who he was... They'd tell you straight up... Everybody respected Big E you know. Everybody respected Big E. Everybody respected Big E...

End scene.

#MATTER

KIM
He messaged me

COLE
We haven't seen each other in a while or spoken
The last time was at a concert
She was a little mad at me
Because the mc performed a song with the n word in the chorus
And she saw me sing along
And she never said anything
But after the show
She was cold to me

KIM
He messaged me

COLE
Hey

KIM
I know it's been a while

KIM
He felt like we needed to talk
Needed to clear the air

COLE
Can we sit down for coffee sometime

——————————————

COLE
Sitting down

KIM
I want to ask you what you meant
but I'm finding it hard to ask you

What I would rather do is just tell you
what I think
about what I thought you meant

COLE
I can explain what I meant

KIM
I am sure you can
But can you explain what I read
And what I took it to mean?

COLE

I just meant that we are all comprised of matter
Matter being that essential molecular element of which
we are all built
Ordinary matter like trees and water
Solids and liquids

KIM

But sounds, the voice for example, was not always considered
matter
Matter used to only encompass a select set of solid objects

COLE

But all along, it was all matter

KIM

What happens to matter split? Does it explode and decimate
millions of bodies of color? And whose hands split that matter?
What we are talking about are black lives split, shaken until
they become bombs

COLE

"Their lives, those lives" – it's all ridiculous
We're here – and we can decide the way this is going to go
This doesn't have to – shouldn't be
And we – us – we don't have to ascribe

COLE
An Aside

There was that summer after senior year of high school.
We were both short on credits. All our friends took off. We had
to stick around. We both ended up working at the Library to make
extra cash. We kinda got close that summer. We talked about
books. Smoked joints on lunch break. That was the summer I got
into R&B and I turned her on to some indie rock.
I thought, "man what a cool chick"

There was that one night after our shift. We got those tall cans
and decided to break into the school.

We heard someone – so we ducked into the only open room
we could find. The Chemistry room. It was dark in there and
we were super quiet...we drank more and started to get close.
Maybe it was because things were coming to an end. We got close
to... but we didn't – she stopped suddenly – said she had to go home

---

#MATTER

COLE
We are on the same side Kim

KIM
Are we?

COLE
Yes! We want the same thing

KIM
After another man is laying in the street
Your immediate impulse is to correct me – to talk semantics with me
To say *Well, actually Kim...*
I don't know what side that is

An Aside

In particle physics, antimatter is material composed of antiparticles;
which have the same mass as particles of ordinary matter but have
an opposite charge

———————————————

COLE
I don't think anyone is less or more
Or special

KIM
When we say BlackLivesMatter
Do you think that's us saying we're special?
"Look at us?! We're getting shot–"

COLE	**KIM**
No but it's sort of making	
your suffering worse than others	
Wait – that's not what I mean	Uhm...what did you just
It's saying your suffering is –	
I mean – what about in Africa –	
all the Boko Haram stuff	
Or women all over the world	
being assaulted	
Or Gays and Lesbians	Okay but we're....
Hispanics being deported,	
shot at border crossings	
Or hell, even poor white folks	
who live in black communities	
Who're bullied because of	
the crimes of others	Cole... Cole...

And and and
I'm all for civil rights but looting?
Property damage and just rage?   No-No-No
It doesn't work –
I mean – it's not strategic   You don't…
All lives KIM
That's all I am saying – let's pull
the act from the context of race
We have to break this down to the root
Human wickedness

KIM
And sometimes humans kill humans because of their race

(A breath.)

COLE
How are we supposed to get anywhere when we can't even get
past this?

KIM
Are you willing to decrease your mass – because that's what it will take
Some stepping aside – but yall don't wanna cede –

COLE
Yall who?

KIM
You keep talking about equality – equality this and equality that but
COLE we're not equal.

COLE
Yes we are

KIM
Black and White. All matter. Is not equal
Different mass
Different volume
Different uses
The water
The tree
Are not the same

COLE
We grew up the same way

KIM
But the way we are perceived is different

#MATTER

COLE
But that doesn't mean those perceptions are true

KIM
Why can't you say it?
Black
Lives
Matter

COLE
Do white lives *not* matter?

KIM
Nobody is saying what *doesn't* matter

COLE
But it's – exclusionary

KIM
It's contextual – in this climate – it relates to the splitting of black atoms

COLE
I *can* say it

KIM
But not without addendum

(A breath.)

COLE
Wouldn't it be great if –
I just wish we could move on. Be ourselves–be individuals – our own
perfect stars – just be our own perfect stars–

KIM
What're you talking about?

COLE
When we were kids – when we'd have a block party all the kids
would be out – getting our faces painted like Spider Man – bike races
– we were just–kids in the neighborhood. When did we start –

KIM
I was the only black kid at that block party

COLE
We were all just kids. Just kids.

KIM
No we weren't all *just* kids. I was the *only* black kid

COLE
I didn't see it like that

KIM
You didn't see I was black?

COLE
I didn't treat you different
Call you names
I didn't spit on you

KIM
But not everybody was like you

COLE
Did somebody spit on you?

KIM
You think just cuz you're enlightened enough
To not be a racist white guy who spits on black people
That everyone else is too – everyone else *must* be the same

COLE
An Aside

She wasn't always like this

KIM
An Aside

I was silent. I used to be silent.

COLE
She used to be real easy going. A cool chick.

KIM
I used to hold my breath. Breathe shallow. Up here in my chest.

_____

COLE
You're my friend

KIM
I'm your black friend

COLE
So does that make me your white friend?

KIM
You just get to be a perfect star

#MATTER

COLE
What I am is legacy
Racist till proven otherwise
No matter if my family did or didn't own slaves
Did or didn't vote a certain way
It's all stamped on my matter

(Continues.)

COLE	KIM
	Oh Boo fucking hoo.
	The white man's oppression!
Wait you...	Nobody is locking you up
	in astronomical numbers.
	Taking away your right to
	vote and then telling you
	to pull yourself up by your
	boot straps
Alright. But...	Nobody has historically
	benefitted from the
	systematic demise and
	oppression of you and yours
	What's the white man's
	oppression? People's mea
	opinions?
I never...	The black comedian's
	caricature? People asking
	him to be politically correct?
	People calling him out
	for hiring his buddies?
	The white man's
	oppression comes in the
	form of screaming voices
	under his foot

COLE
An Aside

I really want to leave. I feel sick.
I want to hug Kim. And tell her I'm sorry
but also – if I'm being honest
tell her to get over it.
life is hard and there is no measuring stick for suffering.
She can change this – just by being her self – not this angry black woman

KIM
An Aside

I really want to let Cole off the hook. Drop this whole thing.
Tell him it's all good. But I have swallowed myself so many times
to make white folks feel less uncomfortable.

COLE
I just want to fix it.

KIM
Cole wants to know how we fix it. Wants me to tell him but
I just woke up this way. I don't know how to dig into the hearts,
rewire the circuitry? Who does? All I am trying to do is keep it
together.

COLE
I want to tell her I am sorry.

KIM
I don't need apologies. I just want it to stop.

COLE
I couldn't say it actually – hurts to say–fills my stomach with all this
history. To say it – is to admit – that – my life – in someone's eyes –
people living, people dead has mattered more than other folks'.

And I don't think it does – but someone at some point has believed
that – and maybe my life has been better because of that –

_____

KIM
That night in the Chemistry room – when we got close –
Cole and I all those years ago – I was into it–I liked him –
until he put his hands in my hair.

I thought about all those kids in school always asking to touch it.
Can I touch it.
And how they'd react when they did. And he had his hands in my
hair and I wondered how he thought it felt. Weird? Funny? Good?
Then I thought about if he'd been with any black girls before and it
was too much so I told him I had to go home. So I did. I left and that
was the closest we ever got.

KIM exits.

COLE
Week or two later I sent Kim a message. I thanked her for
the conversation. I told her we should be in touch more often. That I
wanted to keep talking. Not just about this. But our lives in general.
...and then I got a message back...it was from Kim's mom. There'd

26

#MATTER

been…an accident… …a fucking … …a story…the same story…
again… …the same thing…a misunderstanding…they called it…
a failure to comply…she failed at being silent…so she was made
silent…and I'm left wondering if it's true that life…a spirit or a soul
I guess…has mass.

Does the voice linger – Is it there hanging in the particles?

On her wall
I typed a hash tag
And three words

BLM

by James Austin Williams

MELVIN

Late fifties to early sixties African-American, dressed in work clothes including florescent vest and hard hat. He is at the end of his workday grabbing a bite before heading home

DANTE

Early to mid-twenties dressed in non-branded athletic wear [hoody & sweatpants with a Black Lives Matter shirt underneath] (we shouldn't be able to tell if he is a college student, a banger or a neighborhood youth)

Setting: (fast food restaurant ala MacDonald's, Hardee's or even better White Castle)

Time: (pre-lunch rush at that time just before breakfast switches over to lunch)

NOTE

If I could want to apologize to every black person in America under the age of thirty. I've been functioning under some bad intelligence. *(Pause.)* I believed I could make it better, I thought, if I made more money, moved you into a better neighborhood, sent you to their school you'd be safe. Or at least wouldn't have to go through the things I did. You'd never know the discomfort of having to lock your doors at night, or hear gunfire in the night, then in the evening and finally all times of the day. I wanted you to grow up in a loving environment, surrounded by friends and caring neighbors. You see I believed… I believed that after all the marches, the sitting-ins and boycotts that brotherhood was possible.

OFFSTAGE VOICE Morning can I take your order?

MELVIN Gimme a minute, would you please?

OFFSTAGE VOICE Okay.

MELVIN *(On phone.)* Hey baby. Look I'm running late I got hung up in traffic. Yeah BLM was blocking 14th street, yeah TV cameras and everything. Look don't get me started. I stopped at the burger joint, you want anything? How about Jabre? Ok, turkey burger for you, extra cheese and Dijon on both sides of the bun and chicken nuggets for Jabre and a Dr. Pepper very little ice. Cool, see you shortly. *(Looking up at imaginary menu then to himself.)* I know you ain't gonna like it Denois, but I'm getting me a double bacon supreme. I can't take no more of that turkey crap I don't care if it is good for me. The only real question is; do I want to supersize? *(Looking over counter.)* Can I get little help here!

DANTE *(Enters and stands behind MELVIN leans from on side to the other looking for someone then finally.) (Yelling.)* Anybody here? *(To MELVIN.)* Damn man, I thought this was supposed to be fast food. *(They share a laugh...... After a few beats.)* Excuse Pops, you mind if I step ahead of you? I gotta pick up a pretty big order and I'm kinda in a hurry

MELVIN Yes, I mind! You ain't the only one with things to do and I ain't your damn Pops. Sorry youngblood, it's been a long morning.

DANTE *(Avoiding escalation.)* No offence my brother. *(Settling in, unzips sweat shirt to reveal shirt reading Black Lives Matter.)*

MELVIN *(Seeing shirt.)* Yeah I should a known.

DANTE Excuse me?

MELVIN I said I should a known.

CASHIER: Can I take your order *(To MELVIN.)*

MELVIN Let me get a turkey burger, extra cheese and Dijon on both sides of the bun, a six piece chicken nuggets and a Dr. Pepper very little ice. Oh!......and a double bacon supreme.

DANTE You shoulda known what?

MELVIN That you was one of them.

DANTE One of them......... Really?...... Really?

MELVIN Look forget I said anything it's been a morning and I'm just trying to get home after work and I had to sit in traffic for fifteen minutes because y'all had 14th street shut down.

DANTE *(To CASHIER.)* Pickup for Dante Brooks, I'll put it on my card. *(Gives card to CASHIER.)* Yeah, well sometimes, you got to take a stand

CASHIER This'll take a minute, we switching over to lunch *(Walks away.)*

MELVIN yeah but, it's how you doing it that I don't understand. People trying to get to work or get home, blocking the route ain't exactly the way to win people over

DANTE What would you have us do, nothing? Just let things keep going the way they always have? Look maybe this ain't the time or the place to have this discussion. *(To kitchen.)*
I'll pick that up in the drive thru.

MELVIN No, I been wanting to have this conversation. So enlighten me. Just what is it you want to accomplish?

DANTE I got to pick up this order and get back to the rally so folks can eat. I don't have time to......

MELVIN If you can't explain it to me how you gonna convince white folk?

DANTE I don't think I need to convince you or anyone else of anything but alright, what do you want to know?

MELVIN First of all what do you want to accomplish?

DANTE Well it varies from city to city, just like the needs of every community varies, but primarily we want to put an end to our people dying at the hands of law enforcement, without a system of real investigation, independent of the existing structures that allow us to be gunned down in the street or die in police custody as if our lives have no value.

MELVIN Okay, I can get with that part, it's how you doing it that I don't understand. I mean I don't see no plan, no structure. Y'all just be doing things. It seems like Y'all just be doing things.

DANTE You may not agree with the method but you have to agree that something needs to be done. Right, the fight looks different today because the system is......

MELVIN ...different. You say that like I don't know it. But, you don't work with existing leaders or structures in the community. Seems to me like some you could use some help. There some folk with experience deal inside the system that would be willing to help...... A lot of folks sacrificed, so you could go to better schools, vote and live where you want to live.

DANTE You mean like the politicians, that have sold out our community for their share of condo kickbacks because, they saw they couldn't stop emminent domain from driving us out of our homes for ball parks, or the entrepreneurs and their luxury high rises, so white folks can play safe in their coffee shops and co-ops, with a view of the river. Cause you know white folks love water. Or the mega churches that convinced poor people that their poverty is their own fault because their faith isn't strong enough. After all God wants you to be rich, so you can tithe and get the pastor the latest jet. Maybe you talking about the old guard rights organizations that were on TV every day before Ferguson and Baltimore telling us we need to be respectful, pull up our pants and turn our music down. Like those were the real reasons unemployment is so high for us. Even the president went on TV calling us thugs.

MELVIN And you gone tell me that there ain't no criminal element there? I grew up in that neighborhood, I graduated from Sumner, but I got out of there as soon as I could, I don't go back except for church and after service I get the hell out.

DANTE And that's part of the problem......we know most white folks don't give a damn about us... It's y'all I don't get. You know what's up. You've lived there, you know what happens... Our calls don't get answered as quickly......when the police show up they usually add to the problem acting like everyone is guilty. Listen, I know you get the feeling of dread when the blue lights go on behind you, whether or not you've done anything your fate is in their hands. Really man you've never been stopped for nothing?

MELVIN Yeah, I've been stopped, but I can't say if it was for nothing.

DANTE Did they let you go?

MELVIN Of course I had all of my paperwork in order. License and registration and proof of insurance. Why wouldn't they?

DANTE Did they say why they stopped you?

MELVIN That they were looking for someone driving a similar vehicle.

DANTE So you believed you didn't fit the description but your car did?

MELVIN That what he said.

DANTE And you were okay with that? did they tell you what that description was?

MELVIN They never do.

DANTE And I suppose you're cool with that too. someone stopping you without ever really giving you a reason?

MELVIN It's their job man. If you haven't done anything, then you don't have anything to worry about.

DANTE They ever ask you to step out of the car?

MELVIN No, but if they did......

DANTE Of course not a fine upstanding citizen like you

MELVIN If they did I know the drill, just be respectful, do what they tell you and you can go about your business with a slight inconvenience at worst.

DANTE I see, your parents gave you the speech.

MELVIN And I gave it to my son.

DANTE And he'll give it to his......

MELVIN Well I hope he doesn't have to.

DANTE And that's why we're out there. how old is he? your son......

MELVIN Jabre, he's seven.

DANTE And you gave him the speech already

MELVIN With all the tension you guys are creating...

DANTE *(Cutting him off.)* That we're creating!

MELVIN I don't believe everything the papers say, but stopping traffic on the freeways, disrupting state fairs, blocking people from getting in the stores and malls, you got to know they gon' do something. They got to! You messing with their money!

DANTE They messing with our lives!

MELVIN Not exactly our most valuable citizens.

DANTE Okay, I see where this is going. Criminals, thugs and bangers, right.

MELVIN Like I said, not our most valuable citizenry. If you don't look the part or act the part. pull up your pants, get a job learn to present yourself in a non-threating manner, treat them with the respect and courtesy the office deserves. You shouldn't have a problem.

DANTE What about a twelve-year-old playing with a toy gun in the park? Or a man shopping for toys in a Walmart? Or a woman pulled over for an improper lane change?

MELVIN What about terrorizing a store owner just before, being stopped then resisting arrest, or committing an illegal act in front of a store then resisting arrest or running from the police after being told to stop. Or making gestures that can be interpreted as threatening? All of these are split second incidents.

DANTE And in that split second they always choose to shoot to kill! Yet under those same circumstances white suspects are taken alive. We're not talking about whether they did anything or not. We're not asking for special treatment; we're not asking to be above the law. Law enforcement is killing brothers and sisters of all ages in their houses, in stores, on playgrounds, in vacant lots. Hell, even when they arrest us, we disappear mysteriously or commit "suicide" The law says everyone should get judged by a jury of their peers, but we ain't even making it into the courtroom. You can't tell me you think that's right.

MELVIN I think you have to be able to see a thing from more than one perspective. From what the papers say you've declared war on cops. You shutdown shopping malls, interrupt political rallies and disrupt people's holidays by blocking airports. You'll never win the hearts and minds of people like with those kinds of actions.

DANTE There is no amount of empathy that can duplicate the stress of knowing that as a black person you can be killed simply for being black. In the sixties America saw the footage of our people being brutalized in the south and decided to march against the existing laws. The media has gotten better at spinning stories, putting the focus on the victim instead of the system and since there is no official legislation to be against, people like you buy into it and we accept business as usual.
So every event can be justified with "I was afraid for my life"

MELVIN It's a dangerous job, you have to do thing that most people are afraid to do, run toward the gunshots. You have to stand between society and the criminal elements. Sometimes it's better to ere on the side of personal safety. Sometimes you have to cut corners

DANTE Cut corners, wow! Let me ask you something

MELVIN Go ahead

DANTE When did you decide to turn your back on your people?

MELVIN What?

DANTE Let me put it this way, when did you decide to become one of them?

MELVIN Look, you don't know anything about me, you best back the hell up!

DANTE Didn't you just say something about, how'd you put it. "Not exactly our most valuable citizens". It seems to me that means you think you're better than somebody?

MELVIN Look, I'm not passing judgement

DANTE You say you grew up there, which means your parents' home was there. How much are their lives worth? How much is Jabre's?

MELVIN Leave my family out of this.

DANTE Why? What makes them any different from the families that live there now? See we forget, we get a degree or a better job, gain a little status and we leave. We never look back, we......... how did you put it? "Come back for service then get the hell out". Or we visit Uncle Wes and Aunt Delores on holidays, wonder why they still live there. We become as bad as white folks. we become ashamed and feel like whatever happens to them is their fault because, they don't work as hard as I did. Or they're not as driven as I am so we stop watching the news or become more focused on football, baseball or whatever the hell season it is. You got mad when you saw this shirt because it said Black Lives Matter. When for people like you it should say "My Kind of Black Life Matters" does it really have to be your son or someone you know before you care? because your son is going to have to give that speech to his son, and his son will have to give it to his son, and it will go on that way, if we don't stand up.

CASHIER: Orders up!

DANTE The reason we're there is for too many years sons and daughters have left home one day never to return. Their parents wonder what if they had said just one more thing. Maybe the outcome would have been different, maybe not. Maybe someone cut a corner, maybe not. But think, what if one day it's Jabre. You've worked hard and raised him right. You've given him the talks. But one day he doesn't come home. He fits the description and someone fears for their life and he just doesn't come home. Wouldn't you like to ask whoever is responsible why, and get an answer? Wouldn't you like to see the tape, if one existed? Don't you think everyone should have that right? I've got to get this food back to protest......think about that the next time you're stuck in traffic.

End of play.

OFFICER FRIENDLY

by Rachel DuBose

NINA

30s. Female. Confident

HALIMAH

20s. Female. Anxious

OFFICER FRIENDLY

40s. Male. Aggresive

Time: The present. It's late at the Howard bus stop heading south.

SCENE ONE

Lights up on NINA and HALIMAH as they wait for their bus off Howard.

NINA
(To the audience.) As usual, Halimah of little faith is freaking out about the bus. I get it, she has a "Netflix and Chill" set up.

HALIMAH checks her watch.

NINA *(To HALIMAH.)*
It's coming.

HALIMAH
You said that ten minutes ago. This is bullshit. We should just take an Uber.

NINA
I don't have Uber money. And I don't want to borrow any from you, either.

HALIMAH
Girl...

NINA
It's not that deep.

(To audience.)

For me, at least.

HALIMAH
(To NINA.) Shit, there's a cab.

HALIMAH extends her arm and turns to NINA.

NINA
I'm good. I'll see you tomorrow.

HALIMAH
Sure?

NINA
I'll text you when I get home. Okay?

SCENE TWO

HALIMAH nods and exits.

NINA
(To Audience.) I'm doing what I usually do –

(She puts in her earphones.)

And turn on my favorite Star Wars Podcast. You know, minding my business when –

A flashlight shines into NINA's face. She takes out her earbuds.

OFFICER FRIENDLY
WHAT ARE YOU DOING? WHERE ARE YOU GOING?

NINA
(To audience.) Now, I must have a dumbfounded look on my face because he felt the need to say it again –

OFFICER FRIENDLY
WHAT ARE YOU DOING? WHERE ARE YOU GOING?

NINA
I'm going home, sir.

(To audience.)

I'm trying to show some sort of respect, even though I don't think it's wholeheartedly earned.

OFFICER FRIENDLY
So, you don't live over here? Where do you live?

NINA
Not far.

OFFICER FRIENDLY
Where are you coming from?

NINA
Work.

OFFICER FRIENDLY
Where?

SCENE THREE

NINA
Is there a problem, sir?

(To audience.)

Clearly, my small frame and my "non-threatening" plaid shirt and Converses is a problem.

OFFICER FRIENDLY
What are you doing out here so late?

NINA
I'm coming home from work.

(To audience.)

I'm looking at him and I'm trying to get his name and badge number. Conveniently, both are non-visible.

OFFICER FRIENDLY
Where do you work?

NINA
(To audience.) Now at this point, I'm getting irritated and want him to leave me alone. And I debate poppin' an attitude or letting this shit slide.

(To OFFICER FRIENDLY in a sarcastically sweet tone.)

Why does it matter?

OFFICER FRIENDLY
We got a call there was suspicious looking character roaming around.

NINA looks around.

NINA
We?

OFFICER FRIENDLY
My partner and I.

NINA
Where's your partner?

OFFICER FRIENDLY
I'm the one doing the questioning. You got it? And I asked you, where do you work?

NINA
I work in office in Evanston.

SCENE FOUR

OFFICER FRIENDLY
Doing what?

NINA
It's late. And I just want to get home.

OFFICER FRIENDLY
Sounds like you're being insubordinate.

NINA
We had an office party.

OFFICER FRIENDLY
Can anyone verify that?

NINA
Everyone is gone for the night, "sir".

OFFICER FRIENDLY
Am I sensing an attitude?

NINA
(To Audience.) Yes.

OFFICER FRIENDLY
Do we have an attitude problem? I hope we don't have a problem here.

The OFFICER readjusts.

NINA
No, sir. We do not have a problem. I'm just waiting for the bus. I've done nothing wrong.

OFFICER FRIENDLY
I'll be the one who decides whether or not you've done something wrong. What bus are you waiting for? How far away do you live?

NINA
(To Audience.) The questions are coming a mile a minute. I can't even answer the one before he asks another.

OFFICER FRIENDLY
How long have you've been waiting for your bus?

A beat.

SCENE FIVE

OFFICER FRIENDLY
Did you hear me?

NINA
(*Softly.*) Not long.

OFFICER FRIENDLY
Excuse me?

NINA
Not that long.

OFFICER FRIENDLY
What bus are you waiting for?

NINA
(*To Audience.*) Of course we have a problem. I'm minding my business. I've always had respect for law enforcement, hell my father was a cop for twenty years.

(*To OFFICER FRIENDLY.*)

I've heard you loud and clear. I'm waiting on the 22. It's far enough where walking isn't an option. My bus will be here in less than ten minutes.

OFFICER FRIENDLY
See, was that so hard? Have you seen any suspicious characters?

NINA
No.

OFFICER FRIENDLY
Do you know what I mean by suspicious character?

NINA
(*To Audience.*) Does that mean anyone that's a non-white male?

(*To OFFICER FRIENDLY.*)

I don't think I do.

OFFICER FRIENDLY
You know what I mean? Suspicious. Saggin' pants, expensive shoes –

NINA
Sorry, I don't.

A moment.

SCENE SIX

OFFICER FRIENDLY
You're pretty.

Silence.

OFFICER FRIENDLY
I said you're pretty. That's a compliment. You should say thank you when someone pays you a compliment.

NINA
Compliments aren't free.

(To Audience.)

And this is where it turns. I'm praying to the universe for my bus to come in the next minute–

OFFICER FRIENDLY waits for a second then –

OFFICER FRIENDLY
Alright, I guess we're done here. You have a good night.

OFFICER FRIENDLY exits. NINA sighs and puts her earbuds back in. OFFICER FRIENDLY returns.

OFFICER FRIENDLY
I should wait with you.

NINA
(Taking the buds out.) I'm fine.

(To Audience.)

Everything that can possibly go wrong is going through my mind. Is anyone watching, what's to stop this officer from further abusing his power. I know that anything is possible. Anything can happen. And to think –

OFFICER FRIENDLY
I wouldn't feel comfortable letting a lady wait at the bus stop by herself.

NINA
I'm fine, really.

OFFICER FRIENDLY
Where did you say you lived again?

NINA
Not too far.

SCENE SEVEN

OFFICER FRIENDLY
I can always give you a ride.

NINA
I prefer to take the bus.

OFFICER FRIENDLY
There's a lot of unsavory people on the bus. Especially so late at night.

NINA
Are you done questioning me?

OFFICER FRIENDLY
Maybe.

NINA
The bus is fine.

(A beat.) Isn't your partner waiting for you?

OFFICER FRIENDLY
She's taking a break.

(A moment.)

Do you always work this late? No one to wait with you?

NINA
Tonight, no.

A moment.

OFFICER FRIENDLY
I'm just trying to make conversation.

NINA
I'm okay.

(A beat.) What's your name, officer?

OFFICER FRIENDLY
I didn't tell you my name?

NINA
No. You didn't.

(To Audience.)

I'm sure he knew he didn't tell me his name.

SCENE EIGHT

OFFICER FRIENDLY
You can call me Officer Friendly.

NINA
Excuse me?

OFFICER FRIENDLY
Officer Friendly. You think you can remember that?

(He walks in closer.) Officer Friendly. Spelled F-R-I-E-N-

NINA
(To Audience.) At that moment, the bus pulls up. I've never been so happy to see CTA. I try to hurry and board the bus. He grabs my arm.

OFFICER FRIENDLY
(Handing her a card.) If you're ever out here late at night you should give me a call.

OFFICER FRIENDLY exits. NINA watches him leave.

NINA
(To Audience.) Every now and again, I see Officer Friendly when I'm waiting. I usually hail a cab soon after.

Lights fade.

CALL AND RESPONSE

by Becca C. Browne

CLAIRE

20s. Black woman. She looks like she forced herself to be put together.

GIRL

Black. Her age is flexible. She may either be seven years old or at the age Aiyana Stanley-Jones would have been if she were alive at the time the play is staged. Something about her should be like a seven year old. Something about her should be wise beyond her years.

BRIANNA

Black woman in her late 20s/ early 30s. Black Lives Matter protest leader.

CROWD

The audience, and up to three on stage. Various age/gender/race (preferably people of color).

Time: Now

Place: A park in the city where the play is staged. (In Chicago, I suggest the benches overlooking The Great Lawn in Millennium Park.)

AT RISE.

CLAIRE sits on a bench. She has a loaf of bread with her. She takes a moment to look for birds in the surrounding park. She throws a small piece of bread on the ground in front of her and looks around with exaggerated expectation. No birds appear. She does this about three or four times to no avail, each time trying a new way of throwing the bread piece as if it will conjure the birds to her. Bread pieces are scattered everywhere. She slumps on the bench and starts eating the rest of the bread.

A small group of protestors pass the bench (perhaps coming from aisles in the crowd), holding Black Lives Matter signs, etc. Someone says "C'mon y'all we're supposed to meet over there!" Someone else says, "Why is all this bread here? The fuck?"

CLAIRE watches the group go by, she stands and nearly follows them, but instead plants her feet. She nervously clenches and unclenches her fists, unsure of whether or not to take a step forward. She doesn't notice the young GIRL who has taken a seat on the bench when the protesters passed.

GIRL
You're not going to the march today?

CLAIRE
(Taken by surprise.) Who me? Um, I was thinking about it…but… I don't know.

GIRL
My grandma is out there with them.

CLAIRE
So – shouldn't you be with her?

GIRL
I'll go over there soon, but I'm always with her. Why do you have a loaf of bread? *(She gestures to the bread.)*

CLAIRE
I was trying to feed the ducks –

GIRL
In a park without a pond?

CLAIRE
I mean the birds. *(Beat.)* My sister Della and I used to feed the ducks together when we were kids. I thought, hell, even if there isn't a convenient, unpolluted body of water here, I might be able to feed some birds. And I didn't want to go downtown because those pigeons are abominations…but now I guess I'm left lugging around

a whole chunk of bread. *(Beat.)* Are you hungry? You can have some, I just don't have anything to go with it.

GIRL

You'd rather be here pretending to feed ducks than out there marching?

CLAIRE

It's silly, I know. I wanted to do something *normal* again.

(GIRL gives CLAIRE a "you're bat shit crazy thinking feeding invisible ducks is normal" look.)

CLAIRE

Well! It *used* to be normal anyway.

GIRL

You should really go to the march.

CLAIRE

No. I can't. It's just too

CLAIRE and GIRL

Painful.

CLAIRE

(She nods.) I think what they're doing is great and it means so much and it's important but I... I just don't have the energy. Every day it's something new, someone else.

CLAIRE and GIRL

With skin like mine, hair like mine, eyes like mine.

CLAIRE

I used to go all the time. We both did, Della and I. Fighting and yelling and demanding.

CLAIRE and GIRL

Uplifting, empowering, struggling.

CLAIRE

The list of those slain too long in my head to keep track. We say their names, but they blur in my mind, rush too fast in my veins. And it hurts. But then... I had my sister. *(She notices that she's been cradling the bread in her hands.)*

GIRL

And now...you don't

CLAIRE

She was so reckless, you know, when we were kids. Always trying to climb the tallest tree to get closer to the birds she was so inclined to feed. I'd say "Della that's too high!" Oh, but she wouldn't listen. No,

CLAIRE and GIRL
She would shake her head, beaded braids click-clacking in defiance, beaming with all the pride and ambition she could hold

CLAIRE
and say, "Nah Claire, I won't fall! Just trust me! Trust me, I'll be alright." And I believed her. And every time she was right and she was safe. *(Pause.)*

CLAIRE and GIRL
We went together like peanut butter and jelly.

CLAIRE
Through thick and thin.

(Beat.) Six months ago she was murdered.

CLAIRE and GIRL
An officer.

CLAIRE
Who swore to protect and serve

CLAIRE and GIRL
Yet always made me feel unsafe.

CLAIRE
Like a threat.

GIRL
Like a demon.

CLAIRE and GIRL
Like a thug.

CLAIRE
I'll spare you the details. I lost her. And all I have is this bread without any fixin's.

GIRL
No peanut butter or jelly. *(She begins to pick up the pieces of bread on the ground. CLAIRE watches her.)*

CLAIRE
I haven't been to a protest since. Rising each morning to the pain of reality makes me weary. As if I haven't rested in 400 years.

(Pause.) And sometimes I think I'd rather be numb. I'd rather be asleep than awake.

GIRL
If there's one thing I know, it's that being asleep won't protect you.

CALL AND RESPONSE

CLAIRE
But at least I could pretend.

GIRL
Pretend like nothing is happening?

CLAIRE
Yes! It gets overwhelming – day, after day, like a weight on my back, chains on my heart.

GIRL
(Having finished picking up the pieces, she sits back on the bench with CLAIRE.) Ignoring the burden doesn't make it less heavy. There are people out there – *(Pointing to the audience.)* right there – ready to help you carry that weight. When it gets too heavy, ask for help and you'll get it. *(She offers her hand to CLAIRE. CLAIRE gives her the bread.)*

CLAIRE
I'm supposed to be able to handle it, like she did.

GIRL
And suffer in silence?

CLAIRE
It's better than talking about it. *(Beat.)* I'm exhausted.

GIRL
We all are. Not everyone can be out there, but you can.
Don't let them stop you.

CLAIRE
They already did!

GIRL
You still have us. Waiting for you with open arms to come back.
We are right here with you, holding you up, fighting with you every step of the way. When you find yourself without energy, turn to us for strength.

CLAIRE and GIRL
You are never alone.

CLAIRE
How can you say all this? You're so young.

GIRL
You have to grow up fast to survive in the world you live in.

CLAIRE
Oh honey. *(Beat.)* I wish you didn't have to grow up in a world like this.

GIRL

You have no idea how much I wish I could. I want you to go to the march with me.

CLAIRE

I don't know...

GIRL

Della wants you to go today. It will hurt, but it will help you heal.

CLAIRE

I'm scared.

GIRL

I know.

(The GIRL places the bread in CLAIRE's lap. Their hands overlap each other. There's trust and compassion.)

CLAIRE

Will you tell me your name? I can't go and meet your grandma without knowing that – I'm not searching for whoopin' on top of everything.

(Another small group of protesters heading to march passes by. They stop in front of the bench so that the audience cannot see the GIRL or CLAIRE. They are facing the audience. One of the protestors stops to address the audience.)

BRIANNA

I'm sorry to stop us y'all, but I just wanted to say this. Aiyana Stanley – Jones

CROWD

We say her name!

BRIANNA

Aiyana would have turned fourteen this year*. She was seven years old when a Detroit Police officer came into her grandmother's home and shot her in the head while she slept. His charges were dropped January of last year**. With so many loved ones lost and people to remember, I just want us to remember her today especially. That cop killed her dreams and we CANNOT continue to let this happen! She is with us today. *(Beat, then singing.)* Mama, mama can't you see!?

---

*Aiyana would have been fourteen at the time this play was written in 2016. Her age – and this line – will vary depending on the year it is produced.

**Adjust line as needed to fit the time of production.

CALL AND RESPONSE

CROWD
Mama, mama can't you see!?

(BRIANNA starts leading the CROWD away.)

BRIANA
What the system's done to me?

CROWD
What the system's done to me?

(We hear BRIANNA's lines as she walks off stage and they fade away.)

BRIANNA
It is our duty to fight for our freedom! It is our duty to win. We must love each other and support each other.

BRIANNA and CLAIRE and GIRL
We have nothing to lose but our chains.

CLAIRE
Let's go.

(AIYANA says nothing.)

CLAIRE
C'mon! Let's go, I want to fight.

GIRL
(Who we now see is AIYANA. She's almost shocked. Like she hasn't heard someone call her name in very long time.) My name.

CLAIRE
Your –

AIYANA
My name. Say my name.

CLAIRE
(Pause.) Aiyana.

(AIYANA stands. She walks triumphant through the CROWD as CLAIRE says her name, beginning at a whisper, rhythmically and desperately.)

CLAIRE
Aiyana. Aiyana. Aiyana. *(Repeat as necessary.)*

(When AIYANA is off stage, CLAIRE takes another look at the audience. She soaks them in.)

CLAIRE
I will rest when we are free. *(She exits in the direction of the march.)*

End of play.

BLACK GIRL IN BATHTUB

by Marsha Estell

TASHA

Black 14, developed early, pretends to be 16, and is
a "know it all", but deep down she is just as confused
and scared as Nia

NIA

(Songbird the one) Black 14, shy, just at the beginning of
learning who she is. Smart, but wants to be cool and popular.
She is a strong singer

Setting: Chicago, Illinois, Early 2000,

A very large bathroom of a luxurious Penthouse Condo.

Note: (Acapella Music genre is in the style of R. Kelly,
(Chicago steppers's music) lyrics are original by author of play

(Lights up on a luxurious white bathroom. A large bathtub stands in the middle of the room, off center is two stools and mirrored vanity. TASHA and NIA are dressed in baby-doll lingerie. NIA is seated, Steppers music plays, (R. Kelly style) they bounce along to the music, as TASHA applies make-up on NIA. the music is so good, TASHA dances, NIA joins in

TASHA/MIA

(Sings R. Kelly stepper style.) Crooner coming to your home town
Gather round, gather round
Girl
I'll cast a spell on you
Make you forget your name
Love you all night long
Then I'm gone
Awh don't cry sweet thang
(NIA steps, music ends, she still dancing.)

TASHA

Look at you, who taught you how to step?

NIA

My mama! This ain't my favorite

(She steps with an imaginary partner.)

(Sings stepper style.) All the troubles in the world
Blame the girl
When the timing ain't right
Blame the girl
When she steps out of
Line_____
Just Rewind,
It's your world,
blame the girl

TASHA

You can really sing! *(Looking at mascara tube.)* ...oh shit Mia, you brought the wrong mascara, it's not waterproof, it will run, and we gonna look like zombies when the room steams up. Ooooh, look at you, you look so pretty in your pink teddy, most people think black or red is sexy but I likes hot pink, it looks good on your skin tone. Look just like a Barbie doll, wish I had skin like you. I knew you looked familiar, I think we went to the same grade school, but I'm older –

NIA

You sixteen?

TASHA
Yep. Me and the crooner are the same sign... Capricorn. Want another shot of Hennessey?

NIA
No, it burns –

TASHA
First time burns...second time smooth. Lately, it doesn't agree with my tummy.

NIA
That's why you eating crackers?

TASHA
(She nods.) I can't believe, you didn't see me riding in that pretty ass Benz, I'm waving and waving, and you acting like you didn't recognize me –

NIA
You had on a lot of make-up.

TASHA
Did you think I was Beyonce?

NIA
No.

TASHA
He kept whispering she the one, she the one. We almost missed you, just came from the MAC store..

NIA
I love MAC!

TASHA
I remember you from the neighborhood. He all like stop the car, she the one. You got the same cute face, awh look at Mia's dimples.

NIA
It's Nia...uhm means purpose,

TASHA
That African or something?

NIA
It's from the Kwanza Celebration. You know the seven principles Umoja means unity, Kujichagulia means self-determination and NIA is the fifth day, it means purpose –

TASHA
– Tasha is just Tasha, it don't mean nothing.

NIA

Is it short for Natasha?

TASHA

Eeew hell nawh.

(TASHA turns on water, checks temp.)

NIA

Wow...this bathroom is bigger than my living room. *(Peeks in bathtub.)* You could drown in there.

(TASHA opens fancy bubble bath.)

TASHA

Not me, my daddy taught me how to swim...plus I can hold my breath longer that anybody –

NIA

Uhm I don't think I can do this –

(TASHA sticks bubble bath bottle under NIA's nose.)

TASHA

Nice ain't it? Victoria Secret's pear. *(Pause.)* This is my favorite room, all white like heaven. And this chandelier, over the bathtub is exquisite! Don't tell anybody, but I'm gonna get a P.T Cruiser,

NIA

That old timey looking car?

TASHA

It's what I like, and he's gonna buy it.

NIA

For reals?

TASHA

Yep. Now hold still please –

NIA

You should be a make-up artist!

TASHA

I got skills right? Got it from my uncle-aunti Leona

NIA

(Laughs.) Uncle what?

TASHA

Yep he a drag queen, don't tell anybody, he only dress like that when he come up on the northside...my momma think she taught me how to do a perfect cat-eye, but I been knowed how.

BLACK GIRL IN BATHTUB

I'm not going to need to do my own make-up when I become a star bigger than Beyonce or Rihanna –

NIA

I love Rihanna's hairstyles... You sing?

TASHA

Gonna learn how just like I learn how to do everything else. What cha think?

Holds up mirror.

NIA

Wow, I don't even look like myself

TASHA

Just like a Barbie doll.

NIA practices seductive faces in mirror.

TASHA

Still have those cute dimples...but you are missing something –

NIA

When I was little, I used to take my doll's clothes off, and smash Ken and Barbie all together. *(Demonstrates, with hands laughs, then panicky.)* What time is it?

TASHA

You tell your mom what I told you?

NIA

Maybe I should call again, I left my purse in the living room –

She starts toward door, TASHA stops her

TASHA

Best not to. Girl, you sure you said exactly what I told you and casual like – or did you have a shaky voice?

NIA

Casual.

TASHA

Do it.

NIA

What?

TASHA

I'll be your mom, what's your nick-name? Everybody got a nickname whether they like it or not. Sometimes they have one and don't even know it. You remember Pee Pee Paulie?

NIA

No. Oh yeah...he smelled so bad. Flies used to chase him on his bike.

TASHA

I never called him that...just Paulie.

NIA

Me too...but he did smell bad. *(Sings.) stinky stinky pee pee Paulie*

TASHA

I didn't know you could blow like that. Wait till he hears you sing, from now on, I'ma call you "song bird...the one".

NIA

Songbird... I like that.

(NIA continues to admire herself in the mirror.)

TASHA

First, everybody called me "Lil bit", but then I got these...
(Points to chest.) when I was 11 and seem like my mama was mad all the time, dressing me in giant sweat shirts. Everybody started calling me "lil mama, cept my daddy...said I was the best thing that ever happened. Always said, children, are a blessing. He called me sweet T.

NIA

(Laughs.) Sweet Tea?

TASHA

Our favorite drink, not Koolaid, or lemonade. Always, ice cold, even in the winter time...my momma got tired of making it for him...
so he say Sweet T, can you make some ice cold sweet tea for your dear old dad, just like that "your dear old dad", he wasn't old, not even thirty-five...when those whack doctors said they <u>had</u> to cut his leg off!

NIA

For reals...he only got one leg?

TASHA

My daddy's dead!

*(Loud thumping music outside the door. They both jump.
TASHA goes to the door listens, returns she pours a half a shot...
starts to drink, feels nauseous, grabs a cracker, recovers.)*

TASHA

I know! You need a mole...it adds drama...that's what uncle-auntie Leona would say.

BLACK GIRL IN BATHTUB

(She draws a small mole, on NIA's cheek, then starts packing up make-up quickly. NIA grabs hand mirror, she plays with her hair pulling it to one side to the other, admires her face.)

NIA

No shaky voice... I know how to lie, especially to my mama... especially now. She ain't never home...always over her boyfriend house.

(She pantomimes speaking on the phone.)

NIA

"Bonjour Mademoiselle, pardon! I know it's late, but we still shopping...you know how we do, like mother like daughter, shop to you drop and she laughs and laughs...say you right about that, you got that from me. then I say Taylor wanna know can I spend the night can I, Jolie? *(French.)*

TASHA

What?

NIA

I just called her "pretty one" in French...she loves how it sounds – *(TASHA turns off water in tub, adds more bubble bath.)*

TASHA

Oh. How you say "you are stupid?"

NIA

Tue es stupide.

TASHA

Eres stupido.

NIA

You took Spanish?

TASHA

Why you act surprised? French is too stuck up. Bet you could call her a bitch, and she wouldn't know it.

NIA

I think she would.

TASHA

She wouldn't – How you say it?

NIA

Uhm I don't know.

TASHA

I bet it's *(Fake French accent.)* La BitchCHE

NIA

(*Laughs.*) I think it's La Chienne.

TASHA

You should call her that.

NIA

Why would I do that? I mean, she gets me on my nerves sometimes…but –

TASHA

Moms can be a trip, mine always staring at me –

NIA

(*Nodding.*) Oooh mine too.

TASHA

One day, I just straight up asked her, I was on my way out, I was like Ma why you always staring? She looked like she was about to cry, said "Sometimes… I just can't believe my precious baby ain't my little baby anymore".

(*Long silence, TASHA returns to make-up table, touches up mascara.*) There is muffled sound at the door.)

TASHA

La Chienne huh? Wait, you told your mom, you were going to Taylor's house? That ole lanky ashy girl with the coke-bottle glasses?

NIA

She's cute now.

TASHA

Still wearing those glasses?

NIA

Yeah.

TASHA

Too much medicine in those glasses.

(*There is a faint noise outside door, NIA walks over slowly, tries the doorknob, it doesn't turn.*)

NIA

The door is locked.

TASHA

Here. You forgot your shoes. I wish they had these in my size!

NIA

Why is the door locked?

BLACK GIRL IN BATHTUB

(NIA starts to pace.)

TASHA
Put on your shoes –

NIA
Why? I'm not going anywhere, doesn't make sense.

(TASHA pours a shot.)

Why would I get all dressed up, then get in a fucking bathtub?
He ain't gonna get you no P.T. Cruiser, you ain't sixteen.

TASHA
He is, and if you act like you got some sense, he-he could make you
a star, take you on tour with him. He's going in a couple of months.

NIA
You don't have a license…you ain't sixteen, you are fourteen just
like me… I do remember you, we were in the same kinnygarten
class. I want to go home!

TASHA
Calm down, don't be a baby, take another shot of Henney!

NIA
It burns,

TASHA
Take a shot –

(Knock on door, TASHA crosses.)

TASHA
Uhm… Not ready yet big daddy! We tryin to make your birthday
extra special *(To NIA.) (Whispers.)* Listen! You ain't gonna mess up
my good thing you hear? This is the last time, I gotta do this shit…
he promised. Everything's changed now…can't do this no more.
(Firmly.) He took you to Victoria Secrets, got three bags of stuff,
don't forget to pull the tags off so he can't take it back… Drink.

NIA
No.

TASHA
Come on Songbird –

NIA
My name is NIA! I wanna go home, please

TASHA
(Realizing.) Shit…this your first time? Wow. Okay. Okay, don't
cry, uhm…you like Barbie dolls right? Me too, don't tell anybody…

but I still have them, I dress them up, style their hair, little mole...
on their upper lip, and pretend that they could do anything...go
anywhere...even fly, I wish they could...really fly...you know...away.
(Pause.) Nia, out of all those girls, in the mall, he picked you...kept
whispering...she's the one, she is. Look in the mirror, you look just
like a Barbie doll. So pretty...pink really is your color –

NIA

(Crying.) Why-why he locked the door?

TASHA

(Gently.) Shshsh. Listen...when he knocks the third time...
he's gonna come in...okay? And you gonna stand here, put your
hand on your hip just so. And I'll stand over here and hold your
other hand... I won't ever let go, okay? We will be the most
beautiful barbies...anybody has ever seen okay? Okay Nia, don't
cry...your mascara will run. I won't let your hand go –

*(They stand holding hands for an eternity. Then, a knock on the
door, two knocks, third knock...door opens slowly.) Steam starts
to fill up the room. Lights fade on girls holding hands, steam
continues to roll in, filling up the room. Lights change indicating
passage of time. Special on NIA alone, wearing the same teddy,
mascara runs down her face, (Like a zombie.) but she appears
confident. She holds a bottle of Hennessey and a shot glass.)*

NIA

(Sings ballad style.) All the problems in the world
Blame the girl
When the timing ain't right
Blame the girl
When you step out of line
Just Rewind,
It's your world,
Your world
blame the girl

(She addresses the audience.)

NIA

Oh, don't you worry about that, Don't even worry about being
nervous, he likes that you are...innocent, weird huh? You cut the
tags off? Good. You look just like Rihannna, yellow really is your
color. Good thing we went to the MAC store to get our faces done,
cuz I can't do a smoky eye like Tasha. That's one thing she could
do, couldn't sing but her make-up skills were on point! *(Shakes her
head.)* Nobody knows...nobody talks about it. yeah. I heard she was

pregnant. Yep. And well, uhm he didn't want her to be…
you know? *(Long pause.)* After the procedure…she went home,
took a long bath full of her favorite bubble bath. Victoria's Secret
pear, and yeah, cut her wrists or something…but hey I don't really
know, I wasn't there. I didn't see her that much since uhm you know
since I became the "one", *(Shrugs.)* Haters gonna hate. Oh, did I
tell you he's taking me on tour with him. Yep. *(Pause.)* Awwh, your
knees are shaking.

(NIA pours a shot, downs it, pours another, holds it up to audience,.)
First time burns, second time smooth. Pour vous, ma chérie. You
like my French? It means for you. *(Smiles.)* for you Chienne.

Blackout. End of Play.

FOR COLORED STONED GAY BOIS

by Aaron Holland

A Choreopoem

5 Artists, different races, genders, types. To Play All Types.

AT RISE.

THERE'S HUMMING HERE Nondescript tongues.
The Cast in various wigs, sunglasses, and other shelter.

1

I've gotten

2

Dont you love your own kind?

1

I've gotten

3

That's not really true? is it? Nah. I mean we're all gay.
Like who has room to judge.

1

I've gotten

4

ooh Mandingo. make sure the next time I see you, you wear your
Timberlands.

1

I don't own Timberlands

1

The one One Night Stand I had, the guy got off by rubbing
my dreads on his face.
Like I'm some exotic Barbie – or a new packa Remy hair.
I have since cut my dreads.
I've gotten

5

You must want a sugar daddy

1

And yes, Yes I do, but they didnt have to say that cruel shit.
All this time I'm thinking, but I'm –

2

Wait –
it goes back further than that.

1

You see when I was little it was

2

Oh he's so precocious– born to be an entertainer.

FOR COLORED STONED GAY BOIS

1
I got older

5
Well he speaks so well. Born to be an entertainer and what smarts

1
Teenage years it was

2
Well all he wants to do is entertain, there are other things
in the world boy! pay attention.

1
And then, in College it was weird, like,

4
Can I help you?

3
You need some help?

5
Excuse me sir, can I help you?

1
I mean suddenly everyone was so Helpful in a like scooty poot way.
That's how my mom says shady.

2
Scooty pooty. She was all scooty pooty with me. like eel you know?
Just ugly and helpful

1
When did I go from cute to criminal?
Or like a betrayer –
So here's me and my white boyfriend.

There's humming Here.

1
And we go places and sometimes im uncomfortable.
And at first he said

3
That's not true, you're making it up.

1
And we'd go into one of these "cute little boutiques"
And I'd look at all the cute stuff
and of course, everytime, there's the "cute boutique niche racist
shit" section.

That usually is stuff you put in your kitchen, Mammy Towels,
black butler salt shakers, etc.
On time I found the sheet music to a song called "run N-word run"
You see, I was also raised not to use the N word.
But we go and go to these cute little places
And I notice I'm black and I feel really black in them.
and people stare and stare
and I shut up and shut up.
Then one day I said,

ALL
Notice.

3
Notice what, my love?

1
Oh this and that. A million things.

3
Not a million boo. It can't be a million.

1
And we go about our life.
And I don't say anything. I mean, I continue not to say anything.
And maybe two weeks after that he says

3
Oh my God.
You're right.

5
They automatically assume, I'm paying.

4
They only talk to me.

3
They ask me what your name is, when you are standing right there.
As if you're my dog or something.
Oh my God.

ALL
I notice.

3
But now that I notice,
I can't stop Noticing. I overnotice.
What do I do?

FOR COLORED STONED GAY BOIS

1
And I said to him

4
I'm an Artist.

2
I'm Black,

4
and I'm Gay.

5
Possibly in that order.

1
I can't help any of these things.
I've noticed my whole life.

4
What do I do?
I clue you in. Now you can't unnotice.

3
What do we do?

1
These things and affectations that were just a phase in Childhood
become quiet whispers and subtweets in your mid thirties.

2
Unmarried, still.

4
Do we call him an Old Maid?

5
Waistin all that Good equipment –

3
If only he would do such and such and things and things,
then maybe he –

2
MAYBE he could find the right one.

1
Not my job anymore. I'm busy.

2
Cuz all this time I'm thinking

4
I mean they're calling me all these things my whole life
and Im thinking

2
But I'm

5
But I'm

1
I'm just like this dude.

3
This regular like artist dude that likes music and theatre and stuff

1
Why would you stop me on the street in my pink shoelaces
and matching iPhone?

2
like I'm just

4
like, this guy.

5
This regular art guy

3
an Artist.

1
But I notice. My whole life I've noticed, that I can't just be that.
I must be,

2
a black artist

3
a gay artist

4
a black boyfriend

5
a gay cousin

1
that actor friend

2
That gay dude.

FOR COLORED STONED GAY BOIS

3
Never just dude.

1
I notice. So what do I do.
I clue you in.
Now you notice.

1
God what are they gonna say when they find out I like to dress in drag?!
So now we are here,
on the start of some kind of new revolution.

3
For Black people
For gay people
For artists.

1
Which fight do I fight?
Not like I haven't already been fighting my whole life.

2
And I see my friends on TV marching in the streets

4
on Facebook, posting postulations about policy

5
tweeting truths about terrorism

3
and I wonder, where is that in me?

1
You see because I am this regular dude.
and now we're saying stuff out loud, like, "I wish my white friends didn't
always bring up the fact that I'm black everyday" and not just here, like
all over the world is like I wish to become an equal part of the world,
and then we have these holidays, like mother's day which unite us all as
humans and we sort of forget for one day that we're trying really hard
to hate each other, and then the next day Buzzfeed will come out with:
6 things every introvert knows to be true, or how to deal with the fact
that you're an INFJ, and we all begin to once again subdivide ourselves
and choose sides until we're so separated that it seems like we'll break
apart; and then Father's day comes and suddenly we're humans again.
Where is me in that?
Like what does my Art have to say about that?
Another SHOWBOAT REVIVAL?

4

There is no me without my art.

3

so it's with my art that I fight

5

So it's with my heart that I write.

1

I am already tired of the "new fight"
because I've been fighting it my whole life.

3

So if i'm a Betrayer for dating a white man – if that makes me
Brainwashed

2

If I'm on "their" side by saying nothing

5

If I'm not standing for anything so I'll stand for anything

2

Then of course I'll letchu choose.

1

You look at my life.
I'm Tired.

3

You tell me,

1

Which fight do I Fight?

Curtain.

I AM A WOMAN

by Loy A. Webb

WOMAN 1

aka Sapphire

WOMAN 2

aka Tragic Mulatto

WOMAN 3

aka Welfare Queen

WOMAN 4

aka Mammy

AT RISE.

Each WOMAN is standing in a corner of the stage facing the audience. Every woman except WOMAN 4 has their head hanging low. When they speak they are lifeless. Mainly because they were forced to give up their identity and accept someone else's labels. WOMAN 4 stands confident. Assured. She's the rebel. The script will indicate when the other women are alive and full of energy.

WOMAN 1,3
Who are you?

WOMAN 2
I am Tragic Mulatto. Birthed from the womb of mother Africa. Ripped from my mother's breast and forced to live with my abductor. My abductor is responsible for this. This, held down my foremothers and raped them then discarded them like used rags. And everybody hypes me up to brag cause my skin lighter than a paper bag. But what they don't know is, I'll forgo a couple of men yelling... "Aye. Aye. Aye girl." "It's like that? Stuck up light-skin bitch, you ain't cute anyway." To go back in time and erase the pain that created me. But then again, the majority of our race wouldn't exist.

They rotate in the same formation to another end of the stage. In a square. So they just go to another corner. Still standing in a square formation. WOMAN 4 is obviously irritated with doing this.

WOMAN 2,3
Who are you?

WOMAN 1
I am Sapphire. Too loud, too opinionated, too emasculating, too sassy, too manly, too neck rolling, too stubborn, too hard on our brothers, too independent. Too much the reason Kyrie Irving didn't invite me to the all white girl yacht party. In other words...too black. But like Sisphyus, it's the boulder I've been made to carry upon my back. And it doesn't seem like I'll be putting it down any time soon.

They rotate in the same formation, to another end of the stage. WOMAN 4 is growing increasingly irritated with doing this.

WOMAN 1,2
Who are you?

WOMAN 3
I am Welfare Queen. My kingdom is the projects. My court is my six kids, by six different daddies. My riches come from the king of all kings, Uncle Sam. Or at least that's what they think. They don't see that in addition to the check full of pennies, I work my behind off

to provide for my family and still come up short. But the secret is, I am simply the face of welfare, not the body. The body of welfare is the companies that make millions of dollars in profit, yet still get governmental handouts.

WOMAN 3 says this extremely fast.

I'm-not-going-to-mention-any-particular-car-companies-or-banks-that-received-welfare-checks-a-trillion-times-more-than-mine-and-instead-of-buying-Cadillacs-they-take-private-jets-and-vacation-at-spa-resorts.

Back to normal voice.

But that's neither here or there. I can't wait until the day I can resign my throne. I am sick of lending my face, to someone else's body.

They rotate in the same formation, to another end of the stage. WOMAN 4 is over it. She doesn't move. The woman who is supposed to get her spot, bumps into her.

WOMAN 1,2,3
Who are you?

WOMAN 4 doesn't answer.

WOMAN 1,2,3
Who are you?

WOMAN 4 breaks formation and confronts every woman.

WOMAN 4
No, the question my sistahs is, who are you? Why do we continue to accept these labels people place upon us? Stop it. Stop accepting these fucking labels. We have the power to redefine ourselves, by not only declaring who we are, but who we are not. Cause I don't know about y'all, but I'm definitely not nobody's mammy. I ain't ya hood rat. I ain't ya gold digger. I'm not ya chick, chickenhead, pigeon or any other type of bird.

The other women start to come alive, listening to what she is saying.

WOMAN 4
I'm not your –

WOMAN 2
Broad. I'm not your trick. I'm not ya butch. I'm not your jump off. I'm not your yellow bone, red bone or any other type of bone.

WOMAN 4
Tell em girl, what else you ain't?

WOMAN 2
I'm not even your damn female. Do we go around saying…

ALL
Man, these males is tripping.

WOMAN 3
I'm not your heifer. I'm not your hoochie or hussy. I'm not ya shawty. Nor am I your thot.

WOMAN 1
I'm not your b-word.

WOMAN 4
My girl don't curse but I do. She means we ain't yo bitch.

WOMAN 1
Slut or garden tool.

WOMAN 4
She means your hoe.

WOMAN 2
I'm not your tragic mulatto.

WOMAN 1
I'm not your sapphire.

WOMAN 3
I'm not your welfare queen or jezebel.

WOMAN 4
Then who are you?

The women declare the below lines in a celebratory fashion.
Each time with a newness and different declaration of womanhood.

WOMAN 1
I am a Woman.

WOMAN 2
I am a woman.

WOMAN 3
I am a woman.

WOMAN 4
I am a woman.

WOMAN 1
I am a Woman.

I AM A WOMAN

WOMAN 2
I am a woman.

WOMAN 3
I am a woman.

WOMAN 4
I am a woman.

WOMAN 1
I am a Woman.

WOMAN 2
I am a woman.

WOMAN 3
I am a woman.

WOMAN 4
I am a woman.

WOMAN 1
I am a Woman.

WOMAN 2
I am a woman.

WOMAN 3
I am a woman.

WOMAN 4
Let the whole world hear that…

ALL
I am a woman. Black woman to be exact, and nothing less.

WOMAN 4
Maybe not the type you imagine.

WOMAN 2
Cause we ain't reached your mountain top.

WOMAN 1
But let me remix Frederick Douglass for a moment. Judge a man.

WOMAN 2, 3, 4
Strike man, put woman.

WOMAN 1
Not by the heights in which he has risen.

WOMAN 2,3,4
Strike he, put she.

WOMAN 1
But from the depths in which he has climbed.

WOMAN 2,3,4
Strike he, put she.

WOMAN 1
New sentence reads.

ALL
Judge a woman not by the heights in which she has risen, but from the depths in which she has climbed.

WOMAN 4
Me and my sistahs will continue to climb from the bottom of the totem pole in which you have placed us, to the top where we truly belong. See society marks us as the lowest on the totem pole, supposedly because we are weak.

ALL
But the real reason is the strength in our feet.

WOMAN 2
We will climb declaring I Am A Woman, for every black woman that has been stripped of her humanity.

WOMAN 1
For every black woman that doesn't realize that her perfectly, imperfect self is the reflection of God, we climb for you.

WOMAN 3
For every black woman that's a single mother that's doing all she can to provide for her children, we climb for you.

WOMAN 2
For every black woman abused, forgotten and feels that the glass ceiling of failure is unbreakable, we climb for you.

WOMAN 4
For every black woman in America, disillusioned with how we are treated, we'll get to the promise land one day. Follow our lead.

ALL
Keep climbing.

Lights fade. End of play.

THE BOMB

by Lisa Langford

TINKA

African American, female, 20s, protester who is manning
an aid station during a protest over the death of an unarmed
Black teen by police.

EZRA

African American, male, 20s, reluctant protester, Tinka's ex.

Setting: The basement of a housing project where a make-
shift aid station has been set up.

Time: Now

(A basement storage room of housing project. A vinyl-topped kitchen table is lined with gauze and rows and rows of Milk of Magnesia. High in the center of the back wall is a small window, smudged and dirty and cracked, opened out to the street where the protests are. TINKA, 20s, sits anxiously on an overturned plastic laundry basket. She gets up, jumps, and tries to look out of the window at the chaos up and outside.)

(EZRA, 20s, bursts into the room screaming. He has the heels of his hands on his eyes and he is writhing in pain.)

EZRA
My eyes! My eyes!

(He grabs the first thing he gets his hands on, a bottle of water, and splashes his face. This is like dousing his eyes with acid and he screams more.)

My eyes! My eyes!

(TINKA grabs a bottle of Milk of Magnesia and tries unsuccessfully to wrestle EZRA to the ground.)

TINKA
I'm trying to help you! Be still! Let me help you!

(EZRA clocks TINKA, knocking her on her behind.)

EZRA
My eyes! I can't see!

TINKA
The fuck!

(TINKA roundhouses EZRA, landing him flat on his back. She scrambles on top of him, forces his arms away and pours Milk of Magnesia on his face. EZRA winds down and TINK falls off him, both breathless.)

EZRA
(Coughing.) My eyes. That shit burns. That shit is like fire.

(TINKA crawls to the table and grabs a rag. She throws it at EZRA. They don't see each other. They face in opposite directions, involved in their own pain, EZRA's eyes, TINKA's behind from where she fell.)

TINKA
Stupid ass. You don't touch your face. You don't use water. And you don't panic.

EZRA

(Wiping his face.) You sitting in here! I'm out there and you sitting in here! Go out there and let them spray your ass with tear gas then talk about some "you don't panic!"

TINKA

I'm sitting in here because fools like you need first aid – *(Turning and seeing him.)* Ezra?

EZRA

(Looking up.) Tinka?

EZRA and **TINKA**

Oh.

(Beat.)

TINKA

I didn't recognize/ you

EZRA

You look different/

EZRA and **TINKA**

bigger.

TINKA

I'm not fat/

EZRA

No! You look good/

TINKA

I gained weight / but

EZRA

(Flexing arm.) Me, too –

EZRA and **TINKA**

I joined a gym.

EZRA

(Embracing her.) I like you thick.

TINKA

(Breaking his embrace.) What are you doing here anyway?
I thought we was just a bunch of "hoodlums and thugs" wildin' out and calling it revolution –

EZRA

Tink –

TINKA

Ain't you got a comic book to read?

EZRA
Tink –

TINKA
A white girl to take to Applebee's?

EZRA
Tink – he was my cousin.

TINKA
Oh. Oh.

EZRA
Play cousin. Cousin. I knew him. And they left him there.

TINKA
His body.

EZRA
In the street. For hours. Little kids.

TINKA
Playing on the stoop.

EZRA
And his body.

TINKA
In the street.

(Beat.)

EZRA
Fridays.

TINKA
What?

EZRA
White girls don't like Applebees; they like TGIFridays.

TINKA
(Playfully swatting at him.) You so stupid.

EZRA and **TINKA**
I'm sorry –

TINKA
About your cousin.

EZRA
About the white girl.

THE BOMB

(They might be thinking about kissing each other when a loud sound is heard outside. TINKA gets up and jumps, trying again to look out of the window.)

TINKA
Damn!

EZRA
It's so many of them. They got riot gear, rubber bullets. It's so many of them. They started throwing smoke bombs and everybody just took off running.

TINKA
(Beat.) Why you run for?

EZRA
What?

TINKA
Why you run? The police throw some shit at me, I be like *(Throws imaginary bomb at police. It should look like the image from Ferguson.)* unh! Back atchu, motherfuckas!

EZRA
Why would I do that?

TINKA
To fight!

EZRA
They got S.W.A.T. teams with shields and helmets and bullets – did I mention bullets!

TINKA
You gotta be ready for war!

EZRA
I play Call of Duty; that's as close as I get to war!

TINKA
(Sucks teeth.) Yeah, you was always more Martin than Malcolm.

EZRA
That's a logical fallacy.

TINKA
A what?

EZRA
A logical fallacy.

TINKA
Nerd-ass nerd –

EZRA

There's a disconnect between your premise and your conclusion.

TINKA

Ol' debate-team nerd –

EZRA

They were both charismatic men and great orators who inspired social change fifty years ago. Just because Malcolm had the better movie, you dismiss the sum total of Martin's work and use his name to as a put-down.

TINKA

 – punk-ass nerd. That's why I left your ass.

EZRA

You didn't; I left you. *(Beat.)* For a white girl.

TINKA

How's that working out for you? You feed her chicken strips while the police shooting unarmed Black men every 28 hours?

EZRA

Actually, that's not true.

TINKA

Friday's stopped serving chicken strips?

EZRA

No, no, the "every 28 hours" thing – I looked it up online and it wasn't an academic study, the methodology wasn't scientific –

TINKA

You *researched* our slaughter?! Black people getting killed and you up here fact-checking?!

EZRA

I knew you wouldn't understand –

TINKA

Understand what?

EZRA

I want to understand –

TINKA

Understand what?!

EZRA

The body in the street! I know everything else. I read everything else. I studied it: the evolution of slave patrols to police departments, the 1033 program, Stop and Frisk – I know everything! Except why they left his body in the street. Don't you want to know why?

THE BOMB

TINKA
I wanna know "when" – when you gon' stop overthinking shit
and *do* something.

EZRA
I am doing something! I'm here!

TINKA
So am I. Only difference is: I'm ready to die!

*(The door opens and a bomb is thrown in. Maybe it's a round black
ball with the fuse lit, maybe it's sticks of dynamite bundled with a
timer – it's clearly a bomb.*

TINKA jumps into EZRA's arms.)

TINKA
I don't want to die!

EZRA
(Putting her down.) Calm down. It's probably just a joke.

(The click sound of the door being locked from the outside.)

TINKA
It's not no joke, Ezra!

EZRA
The window! Come on!

*(EZRA folds his fingers and makes a step to boost TINKA up to the
window. She tries but can't fit through the window.)*

TINKA
(Steps down.) I'm not fat.

EZRA
It's a small window.

TINKA
You could fit.

EZRA
(Shakes head no.) And leave you here?

(The bomb is ticking.)

EZRA
It's ticking; that's good.

TINKA
It is?

EZRA
Yeah, that means it hasn't blown up yet.

TINKA
Ezra!

EZRA
Okay, okay! *(Thinks.)* Bombs, bombs, bombs. Okay, there's usually a red wire and a blue wire.

TINKA
Uh-huh.

EZRA
And if you, if you cut the…red wire, it diffuses the bomb.

TINKA
Alright! Okay! *(Fishes a nail clipper out of her bag.)*

(EZRA takes the clippers and inches toward the bomb.)

EZRA
The red wire. *(Steps.)* The red wire. *(Steps.)* *(Stops.)* Or is it the blue wire?

TINKA
You don't know? I thought you knew!

EZRA
I do! It's just – The General always cuts the red, but with Firefly, see, it doesn't really matter 'cause his suit is fire-retardant –

TINKA
Comic books! We finta die and you talking about some damn comic books! Talk and read! You don't do nothing but talk and read!

(EZRA wraps his arms around TINKA, more to keep her from freaking out than anything else.

They sink to the floor still in each other's arms. Maybe they squeeze against a wall or put an upturned table between them and the bomb.)

TINKA
Are we gonna die?

EZRA
A bomb in a basement –

TINKA
I don't want to die.

EZRA
– it's been done before.

TINKA
I know what I said, but that's just something you say –

THE BOMB

EZRA
Birmingham. Mississippi.

TINKA
– to show you're down for the movement, like Pac or the Panthers –

EZRA
Newark. '68, Panthers got bombed twice in Newark.

TINKA
You think we'll be a hashtag?

EZRA
#EzraandTink?

TINKA
Why your name gotta be first?

EZRA
#TinkandEzra.

TINKA
Can we have a funeral?

EZRA
Depends on the bomb –

TINKA
My mother would want a funeral.

EZRA
Internal damage, you could have an open casket.

TINKA
And if my brains end up in the parking lot?

EZRA
Memorial service.

TINKA
Together?

EZRA
Why not?

TINKA
The white girl.

EZRA
(*Shakes his head.*) Just a friend.

TINKA
Oh.

EZRA
From my Black Studies class.

TINKA
(*Understands.*) Oh.

EZRA
She said I was all Martin...

TINKA
(*Smiles.*) and not enough Malcolm.

(*They laugh. Maybe kiss. Yeah, kiss.*)

EZRA –

(*EZRA notices the bomb has stopped ticking. It stopped about ten lines back.*)

EZRA
It stopped! The bomb stopped ticking!

TINKA
We're gonna live?

EZRA
(*Moves toward bomb.*) It didn't go off. I think we're all right.

TINKA
We're gonna live! We're gonna live!

(*They get smoochy close.*)

EZRA –

(*Off-stage, the police break the door down and cock their glocks [if glocks cock, I dunno]. This happens fast.*)

POLICE
(*O.S.*) Police! Hands up!

EZRA and **TINKA**
Don't shoot!

(*Breath.*)

BLACKOUT.

(*Boom.*)

End of play.

IN THE LAND WHERE ALL BLACK MEN GO
by Christina Ham

QUINCY
A mother

DAMON
A son

Time: Now

Place: Where we live and breathe

QUINCY's house. Late night.

DAMON
Sky's orange.

QUINCY
We must be in hell.

DAMON
Then, you overdressed.

QUINCY
You youngsters don't know anything about dressing for the occasion.

DAMON
What time is it?

QUINCY
Around midnight.

DAMON
No time for a woman to be running around in these streets.

QUINCY
Excuse me?

DAMON
They've been rioting for three nights now.

QUINCY
It won't do no good.

DAMON
You don't know that.

QUINCY
I know enough.

DAMON
They just want to be heard.

QUINCY
Then, there's better ways to do it.

DAMON
What you expect them to do when no one will listen.

QUINCY
What's going on out there only reinforces why we need more law and order.

DAMON
You talk about them like they're terrorists.

QUINCY
Most of my colleagues think they are. I try to give them the benefit of the doubt, but when I have to go to work on nights like this – it's hard.

DAMON
Why you have to go?

QUINCY
I start my shift in an hour.

DAMON
You could call in sick.

QUINCY
They'd know I was lying.

DAMON
How?

QUINCY
Because they know I'm not that weak.

DAMON
They don't know you like I do.

QUINCY
You're too young to know what you think you know.

DAMON
Is that what you think?

QUINCY
I want you to promise me that you'll go to bed when I leave.

DAMON
–

QUINCY
Lock the door, shut the curtains, close your eyes.

DAMON
I can't promise that.

QUINCY
I need for you to shut your eyes…just until it's all over.

DAMON
I'm already woke. Even you can't make me go back to sleep.

QUINCY
I should've left you –

DAMON
What kind of mother would you be if you had?

QUINCY
–

DAMON
I'm glad you got me.

QUINCY
Don't make me regret it.

DAMON
Do you?

QUINCY
You're my son. I gave you life – even when your father – couldn't. I watched you breathe…every day. I have many regrets because that's what life gives a mother.

DAMON
Does anyone know I'm here?

QUINCY
No.

DAMON
You lying.

QUINCY
A mother's job is to protect her child.

DAMON
Where do they think I am?

QUINCY
Does it matter?

DAMON
It does to me.

QUINCY
They think you're in the land where all black men go.

DAMON
Am I?

QUINCY
You should be asleep.

DAMON
I told you – I'm not sleepy.

IN THE LAND WHERE ALL BLACK MEN GO

QUINCY
The screams outside must be keeping you awake.

DAMON
It's not just the screams…

QUINCY
The crying –

DAMON
Tears are salt – they give this nightmare flavor.

QUINCY
The gunshots –

DAMON
Let me know I'm still alive.

QUINCY
Then, what is it?

DAMON
It's the scent of blood baking on the hot pavement floating into the summer air that's keeping me awake. I don't know where it's coming from.

QUINCY
You must be smelling the slaughterhouse down the street.

DAMON
This kill floor isn't in a slaughterhouse.

QUINCY
This was a respectable community. People used to wave and say "hello". There were the signs that said, "All Are Welcome". The tourists would even drop their lines here and go fishing.

DAMON
You used to let me sell lemonade to them. They were impressed that a young black boy could be so good at math.

QUINCY
But, suddenly people shut their doors and windows and took down their signs. It's been every man for himself ever since.

DAMON
The government took down the signs and those that wouldn't they made them.

QUINCY
Words are empty if it's not written on your heart.

DAMON
You don't have to go along with what they're doing.

QUINCY
It's my job.

DAMON
You can always find another one.

QUINCY
A son telling his mother she can always find another job doesn't know the sacrifices she made to take the first one.

DAMON
It doesn't bother you?

QUINCY
What?

DAMON
That people that look like your son are being murdered in the streets by your co-workers?

QUINCY
I told you if you were ever stopped give them my badge number.

DAMON
Some of my friends get a Bar Mitzvah as a rite of passage, mine is a Terry stop.

QUINCY
Stop it.

DAMON
The truth hurts?

QUINCY
Pain hurts.

DAMON
I should've noticed it before. You don't look nothing like me.

QUINCY
What's the matter with you?

DAMON
My skin's black and yours is blue.

QUINCY
Those men and women in my department watch my back and keep me alive so that I can come home to you.

IN THE LAND WHERE ALL BLACK MEN GO

DAMON
A black son in your line of work is a curse – not a blessing.

QUINCY
Why are you trying to break my heart before I have to go to work?

DAMON
I broke your heart before I was born. You know it and I know it.
The sleepless nights you spent wondering if I'd make it home…
wondering if you'd get a phone call…or see breaking news.

QUINCY
I told you give them my badge number… That was your rite of passage.

DAMON
It's my fault?

QUINCY
I raised you to know you've never had room for error.

DAMON
I wasn't doing nothing wrong.

QUINCY
Anything wrong. Is that how you spoke to him?

DAMON
That ain't the point.

QUINCY
Isn't.

DAMON
We have a right to peaceful protest.

QUINCY
You should've been home – in bed – sleeping. You lied to me…
Cursed be a son that lies to his mother.

DAMON
I'm doing everything right. The cops throw the tear gas and
I remember what Mariam told me: run against the wind and don't
rub my eyes.

QUINCY
You do what some Palestinian woman tells you on Twitter, but not
what your mother's taught you.

DAMON
Sometimes a mother's advice becomes obsolete.

QUINCY
You should've listened –

DAMON
I put my hands up –

QUINCY
I became a cop to protect you –

DAMON
I didn't breathe –

QUINCY
If they knew me, they knew you. My badge number was your badge number.

DAMON
Because if I'm not breathing then I'm not here... I'm somewhere else.

QUINCY
You're here and I'm here with you.

DAMON
I'm drowning... Mama?

QUINCY
Sh...

DAMON
I can't...it's hard...

QUINCY
You're drowning because I never taught you how to swim.

DAMON
My blood... I can't breathe...

QUINCY
Tell me who did this?

DAMON
Enough blame to go around, mama.

QUINCY
You shouldn't have snuck out. You were supposed to do like I said – lock the door, shut the curtains, close your eyes.

DAMON
You have to let me go.

QUINCY
I can't.

IN THE LAND WHERE ALL BLACK MEN GO

DAMON
What good does it do to relive this nightmare? You should've left your memories of me...alone.

QUINCY
My memories of you are the only thing I have left. You can come and go whenever you want. You're more powerful now than you ever have been. Now, men and women gather in your name and they march on behalf of the names like yours.

DAMON
I'm going to do like you said and shut my eyes.

QUINCY
Damon –

DAMON
Go to the land where all black men go –

QUINCY
Wake up –

DAMON
They're waiting on me.

Lights down.

End of play.

THIS BITTER EARTH

by Harrison David Rivers

JESSE HOWARD

Male, late 20s – early 30s, serious, passionate, black

NEIL FINLEY-DARDEN

Male, late 20s – early 30s, beautiful, compassionate, white

Setting: New York City, NY

(Union Square, New York City.
March 2012.
The Million Hoodie March.
NEIL and JESSE speak out.)

NEIL

I don't even remember how I ended up with the megaphone in the
first place
Honestly, I was as surprised as –
I mean, there were *so* many people
So many... bodies, you know?
I'm talking knees
And elbows
And arms
And legs
And everyone was
Pressing in
Like –
(NEIL demonstrates.)
And at one point I looked down
Just like –
(NEIL demonstrates.)
You know?
I looked down
And there it was in my hand –

JESSE

My roommate Rashaad was like, "are you coming to the march?"
And I was like, "what march? Nah – I'm watching fucking Youtube."
And he gave me a look like, really motherfucker? Youtube?
"The Million Hoodie March," he said.
"For Trayvon fucking Martin!"
And clearly my face didn't make the right face
Because he followed it up with
"A seventeen-year-old black boy gets shot on a city street in the
land of the free and the home of the brave and YOU'RE GONNA
SIT IT OUT because you don't think it has anything to do with you?"
I still didn't make the right face
"Nah, nigga. We're going downtown"
And then he literally grabbed me by the arm
Pulled me out of my room
Down the hallway
And to the front door.
"Hold up hold up!
Rashaad, man – I have a thesis to write."

THIS BITTER EARTH

To which he responded
"Jesse, man
You ain't writing yr thesis
You're dicking around."
And I was a little stunned
Because he was serious
And I hadn't known Rashaad to be serious.
Like ever.
"Put this shit on," he said
And he tossed me a hooded sweatshirt.
"Maybe *this* shit'll inspire you."

NEIL
And it wasn't like I had any intention of using it
I mean
Number one
It wasn't mine, right?
The megaphone
Not mine
And number two
I was just there to support, you know?
In solidarity –
But then the guy next to me noticed that I had it
That I was holding this megaphone
And he was like
"Why the fuck aren't you using that thing?"
And I was like
That's a good fucking question –

JESSE
We pushed our way to the park at Broadway and Fourteenth
And the first thing I saw was this white boy climbing up on the
statue of George Washington
And I'm thinking
He's the one with the bullhorn?
He's the one hyping the crowd?
This white guy?
Please
We might all be Trayvon Martin
But we aren't all of us black.

NEIL
So then
All of a sudden
I'm being hoisted up onto the statue
You know the big statute of George Washington on his horse?

Yeah
Well I'm literally being pushed into his bronzed junk
And I'm trying like hell to hold onto the megaphone with one hand
And to wrap my arm around Blueskin's knee with the other
You know, for stability
And the people below me are like
"All right, white boy"
"Let's hear it"
And I'm wracking my brain, you know
Like seriously stressing about what to say
Because the last thing that *this* crowd needs to hear is another
empathetic white person talking about "I feel yr pain – "

JESSE
And this bitch
This bitch with the bullhorn
Starts reciting
For My Own Protection.
For My Own Fucking *Protection* – !

NEIL
And the first thing that pops into my head is this Essex Hemphill
poem I'd memorized for a Queer Lit class my junior year of college –

JESSE
And I'm like
What the fuck do you know about Essex Hemphill?
Like who the fuck are you – ?

NEIL
"I want to start
An organization
To save my life.
If whales, snails,
Dogs, cats,
Chrysler, and Nixon
Can be saved,
The lives of Black men
Are priceless
And can be saved…"

JESSE
And at first I'm pissed
At first I'm like
Here we go again
Yet another example of blatant cultural appropriation
But then –

THIS BITTER EARTH

NEIL
"We should be able
To save each other…"

JESSE
I'm looking around
And the people are…
Well
They're listening –

NEIL
"I don't want to wait
For the Heritage Foundation
To release a study
Stating Black men
Are almost extinct…"

JESSE
They're listening to the words of a virtually unknown black queer
poet GENIUS –

NEIL
"I don't want to be
The living dead
Pacified with drugs
And sex…"

JESSE
And they get it.
They fucking get it –

NEIL
"If a human chain
Can be formed
Around missile sites – "

NEIL/JESSE
"Then surely Black men
Can form human chains
Around Anacostia, Harlem.
South Africa, Wall Street,
Hollywood, each other…"

JESSE
And I'm speaking the words along with him
(I don't even realize I'm doing it at first)
Speaking Essex's words along with the white man with the bullhorn
dangling from the statue –

NEIL/JESSE
"If we have to take tomorrow
With our blood are we ready – ?"

JESSE
"Do our S curls,
Dreadlocks, and Phillies
Make us any more ready
Than a bush or conkaline?
I'm not concerned
About the attire of a soldier.
All I want to know
For my own protection
Is are we capable
Of whatever,
Whenever?"

(Beat.)

NEIL
And then I lowered the megaphone
And it was quiet

JESSE
No one spoke
No one even breathed
I certainly didn't

NEIL
And then –

JESSE
And then –

*(The sound of a roaring crowd
Which becomes chanting
NO JUSTICE, NO PEACE!
NO JUSTICE, NO PEACE...)*

End.

JEZELLE THE GAZELLE

a short play

by Dominique Morisseau

JEZELLE

Black girl, 12-13 years old. Spunky. Sassy. Full of energy and wit. A sprint runner. The only girl in an all-guy crew.

Setting: An inner city neighborhood. Fashioned after NYC but not necessarily NYC.

Lights up on JEZELLE.

JEZELLE
We was runnin' like the wind.

Me, Rasheed, and Spider

Lights up on JEZELLE.

JEZELLE
Reason why we call him that don't match. Cuz he thin and wiry and we was gonna call him Skinny but it's already another Skinny J on the block and you can't do repeats. So we went from Skinny to Spider cuz they both start with the letter "S"? I don't know. Rasheed say it's bad luck to kill a Spider so it's actually increasing his life expectancy for us to call him that so he liked it and it's cool.

We be racin'. Everyday on the block. Spider be third place always, but me and Rasheed be neck and neck. Last race was a tie if you ask me, but Rasheed swear he beat me. That's complete bull but wasn't no witnesses. *"Get some witnesses!"* I told him. So he did. Rematch. This Friday. In front of Skinny J. Rocky. Burnt Skin Ernie. Spider. And that boy from the foster home that nobody knows his name. I'll be the only girl. It's cool, I'm used to it. I'm always the only girl.

Five dollar admission for the big race. That was Spider's idea. I tried to tell him you can't charge people for getting onto their own block. That's like what they did to the Indians and the Africans and whatever. But he say people willin' to pay. And if they willin', then it's stupid not to take it. *If people wanna give you they money, it's like immoral or anti-American not to take it or whatever.* Spider got a uncle on Wall Street, he say. I don't ask nothin' more about it.

The whole block start buzzin'. Race this Friday. Best runners in the 'hood. Come put yo' money down. Winner gets half of the pot. That was Spider's idea too. He say he get to keep the other half cuz chargin' people was his idea. I tell Spider he need to stop talkin' to his uncle or we may have to stop hangin'. For reals.

I'm gettin' that short sprint perfected cuz one day I'ma do Olympics. Gold medal baby. That's the long term. Short term I just wanna beat Rasheed cuz he be crazy shit talkin' all day on some "I'm a girl and can't keep up" ol' skool cave man philosophy. Sometimes you just gotta shut dudes down. I practice at the track after school on my own. He don't be seein' that. He think all he see is all I got. Always gotta keep your opponents under-estimating you. Always.

116

JEZELLE THE GAZELLE

I be tactical with mines. I be stretchin' so I don't pull no muscle. No DQ's. No unforced victories. I'm gettin' mines by pure honor and craft.

Rasheed and me was out for blood. This was him against her. Pre-teen man against pre-teen woman. This is for Equal rights and Democracy. All women and men created equal. I'm like a Civil Rights runner.

Spider was in the middle. Always between me and Rasheed. Always tryin' to get us to stop beastin' on each other. 'Sheed call me *"Just chest Jezelle"* cuz I'm flatchested or whatever. I don't care. I tell him *"If I had big breasts like his older sister Tawnee then I wouldn't be able to run as fast and I wouldn't be able to leave him chokin' on my dust when I run circles around him in the race on Friday!"*

Spider just be sittin' between us. Always between us. Like, *"Chill ya'll. We all family at the end of the day. This block belongs to us. It's home. It's our turf. And we gonna get paid together."* Spider always tryin' to get us to be all PG and cartoon movie and bff actin'. We'd do it. For Spider. We was crew cuz of Spider. Cuz you couldn't say no to Spider. He just so skinny and funny and even though it sound weird to say it out loud (cuz ain't none of us into the mushy and the soft)… You kinda love Spider. Like also maybe fall in love with him.
Like maybe. A little. But I'm too young to know what love is.
So maybe not. And anyway, love is corny. Love will make you lose a race. Game on.

My mama starts callin' Spider Don King Jr. No adults invited to the race, but we all got feelin's that they'll be watchin' from the windows. My mama offers to make me a "Jezelle the Gazelle" t-shirt. I tell her I don't do rhymes. That's corny. But she makes me one anyway. I wear it cuz I don't want her to feel wack. But I hate every bit of wearin' it. She's makin' me like her runnin' baby doll. I got a feelin' she's not takin' this race seriously. This is life or death. This is for Democracy and Equal rights for the only girls on every block. This is for neighborhood pride and respect. This is for real. This is not a game. But Mama makes the shirt magenta. I love magenta. I wear it but I'm not smiling for pictures. A woman's gotta have her boundaries.

Race day comes. It's a weird day. We in school just waitin' for the bell to ring cuz now other folks in class done heard and the $5 pot is up to like $100. I start thinkin' of all the stuff I can buy with $50. I'ma invest it wisely. Won't spend it all in one place. Half will go under the mattress for a rainy day. The other half on a down payment for this new 10 speed I've been eyein' at Greg's Bike Shop up the street. It's magenta with yellow stripes. It's got Jezelle's name all over it. I'ma be rollin' that baby up the block right past Rasheed, like "Whassup yo! Need a lift???"

I tell Spider my bike buyin' plans. He asks me if I'm ready. I tell him I was born ready. My mama said I used to kick her in the belly so hard she thought I was tryin' to break through. She said she knew I had lightenin' in my feet even then. I got this race.

Spider wasn't feelin' good this day. He kept walkin' slow and dragging his feet. He looked like something was type heavy on his mind. I asked him what was up. He wouldn't say nothin'. Just kept lookin' away from me. Playin' it cool. Sayin' he was good as ever. But he wasn't. Somethin' was up. I pinched his neck real hard til' he pushed me. *"Aight aight yo!"* He said. *(Beat.)* *"We gotta move."*

All shit stopped. I thought my heart fell out of my body. I looked around on the ground to make sure.

What? Movin' where?

To Cali, he said.

What for? What's in Cali?

My aunt's house.

Why you gotta go?

My brother's in trouble. Some cops came by the house last night lookin' for him.

He do somethin'?

Nah. But he got these friends and…maybe they did somethin'. My mama said they the wrong influence. She can't take it no more. Said we gotta get out before they take us all under.

Why don't she just send your brother to Cali? Why you gotta go???

Family stick together.

That was all he said. But it sounded like he said a lot more. It sounded like he was saying goodbye forever. I didn't know what to do. I just looked at him for a second. A really long second. Then I just kiss him. Right out the blue. Ain't even sure what came over me. I'm not the kissin' type. I was totally another Jezelle.

JEZELLE THE GAZELLE

Spider kissed me back though. He didn't even act weird about it or nothin'. He just kissed me back and it was soft but not mushy. It was just... I don't even know what it was.

He whispered in my ear, *"You ready for the race?"*

I said *"Yep."*

He said, *"Low key—I want you to win."*

I said *"Good."*

Then I asked him how he was gonna spend his $50. He said if I win, he's gonna put it toward my bike fund...since he's movin' and what not. Like a goin' away present. I started to feel my eyes itch like they wanted to cry. But I didn't. Cuz I never cry.

Not even when my heart is breakin'. I had a race to win.

Ready. Set. We was on the startin' line at the front of the block. Rasheed had gotten his hair cut. He looked fresh and clean. But so what. I had my magenta baby doll runner Jezelle the Gazelle t-shirt. My mama was lookin' through the window and wavin' – CORNY.

Another mama, one uncle, Skinny J's father, and Ms. Jefferson with the blind dog – they was all lookin' out their windows. Ms. Jefferson was on the stoop. But everybody was there. And almost 20 kids from school. This had turned into the biggest race of my life. I stretched my calves. Rotated my ankles. Grabbed my elbow behind my back. No mistakes.

Spider was gonna run too. Just for kicks. Everybody knew he was no match for me and 'Sheed. But he was just runnin' behind us, for ol' times sake.

Burnt Skin Ernie was holdin' the banner at the other end of the block. I was keepin' my eyes on the prize.

Skinny J called it.

On your march.

We corrected him.

On your marks.

Get set.

I was sweatin' now.

GO!!!!!!

We was runnin' like the wind! I could feel myself like elevatin' almost. My lungs was on fire. I could see Rasheed in my peripheral. He was close, but I was pullin' in ahead. All sound disappeared. All I could hear was my own heartrate. My own feet bouncin' against the street.

I got close to the banner. Didn't see Rasheed in sight. It was me! I was in the lead! I pulled in closer. Closer! BANG!

My body tore through the sheet that said WINNER. I looked back to see the crowd cheering. I could hear their voices like sirens.

(Pause.)

But that wasn't cheers. That was screaming. And it wasn't a sound effect. It was real sirens. And Rasheed wasn't on my heels. He was behind me. Far far behind me. On the ground. Not moving. Not moving. Not moving.

And Spider… Spider…wasn't in third place. He wasn't running either. He was on the ground. Not moving. Not moving. Not moving.

And the screams were sirens. And the sirens were screams. And there was a police on foot. And he had a gun. And I couldn't breathe. I couldn't even breathe. And I just sat on the ground. Not a winner. Not anything anymore. Just a runner gasping for air… gasping gasping for air.

(Long beat.)

I never liked DQ's. DQ's are stupid. No one likes winning by default.

(Beat.)

My mama cried and I didn't. She kept shaking her fists in the air… All I could make out was fragments. It sounded like she forgot how to speak in real sentences.

"Those boys didn't do" and *"Just running a race."* and *"Ain't all running from crime"* and *"Didn't nobody hear"* and *"Had the wrong boys!"* and *"Weren't even the same age!"*

I stopped listening and closed my ears. But sirens kept going. All night. All through my dreams. And I couldn't stop running.

(Beat.)

Two weeks after the big race, I went back to school. It was strange without 'Sheed and Spider. Everybody kept askin' me if I was okay. All the teachers kept askin' me if I needed to talk. I didn't say nothin'. I don't know if I'll ever say nothin' again.

JEZELLE THE GAZELLE

My mama came to pick me up. She didn't want me walkin' by myself. Not while things are still so fragile, she said. Not while people are out there upset and confused. They killed Spider and 'Sheed. They were chasin' those boys that hang with Spider's brother. They said they went running around our block. They said they had just robbed a store. Nobody has seen those boys. They must be hiding good. But Rasheed and Spider...everybody saw. And the officers said they yelled *STOP*. Said they yelled it three times. But nobody heard nothin'. We were runnin' a race. Nobody heard nothin'. But everybody saw.

My mama and me walked past Greg's Bike Shop. I saw the magenta 10 speed with the yellow stripes. It was talkin' to me. But I didn't feel like talkin' back.

Mama said – *The students are giving money to Spider and Rasheed's families. Did you want to give anything?*

I said, *Spider raised $100 for the race. I don't want my share. Can that go to the families?*

Mama smiled.

You wanna race me home, Mama asked? I told her I didn't wanna race no more. Mama said, *One day you're gonna have to get back on the track. You can't let this knock the wind outta you forever. You just can't.*

I told her, *Didn't that officer know it's bad luck to kill a Spider?*

Mama didn't answer. She just took a deep long breath, and we kept walkin'.

(Beat.)

I still go to the track. I still perfect my stride. One day I'ma do Olympics. Gold metal.

One day I'ma be able to run without bein' afraid. But somedays still, when my feet are movin' fast and I can hear the wind in my ears, I look back to see who's runnin' after me. I look back to see who's left behind. I look back to wipe a tear from my eyes...even though I never cry...and then I look ahead and keep runnin'. For Rasheed. For Spider. For Equal rights. For Democracy. For the only girl on every block. For Civil Rights. And for everybody still in the race.

On your **march**...get set...

Blackout.

End of play.

SPEAKING FOR THE UNHEARD VOICES

by Reginald Edmund

R

An African American Male

S

A Black British Female

Note: Text written in *italics* indicates the messages received from the other character. Chorus implies that R & S speak these lines together... united.

(In darkness.)

R
Speak for

S
       The Unheard

CHORUS
Voices.

S
       Speak for

R
The Unheard

CHORUS
       Voices
Speak for the Unheard Voices
       Like
Like
       Click
Like
       Share
Share
       Wait
What?
       Comment
Delete
       Junk mail
Click
       Junk mail
Delete
       Open

(The lights focus on a singular figure in the darkness... It's S.)

      S   **R**
Are you there?   *Are you there?*

      S   **R**
I'm here.   *I'm here.*

      R
He says.

      S
Sorry it's taken me so long to message you. I hope you don't hold it against me.
      She says.

R

No worries.

Spotlight on R and S.

R *(Cont'd.)*

He says...

S

*What time is it there? Duh six hour difference. Sorry just googled.
I hope I didn't wake you.*

Awwww...he's so sweet.

R

I was up. So much work to do.

S

I can only imagine

R

How are you?

S

I'm well. And you?

R

*I'm okay ...I'm okay ...
I'm doing alright...*

CHORUS

I just journeyed to my old home in Houston.

S

*It was a weird moment for me.
I visited my old high school in Texas and graffiti'd upon the wall is a
Swastika and the words "Kill Niggas" on it. It makes me think about
when I was a scrawny kid in school and just wanting to fit in and this
boy...this white boy tied a white noose on my backpack as a joke
and I just carried it on my bag through the hallways of the school...*

CHORUS

What?

S

*Yeah...got to love Texas. I just walked down that hallway of the
school with that damn noose tied to my bag. Smiling to hide my
anger. Scared if I show them how hurt I've been by their actions
or responded in someway they'd think I'm not cool or something. I
don't know why I just shared that with you. That's been on my mind
lately.*

R

I'm so sorry to hear that.

S

I'm just trying to make sense of this world. You know?
I feel like as writers it's our duty to serve as politicians and preachers,
hell even prophets...
And I just keep thinking that I'm a playwright and yet I don't have
the ability to speak for the unheard.
What sense does that make?

_____

R

Speak for

    S

    The Unheard

CHORUS

Voices.

    S

    Speak for

R

The Unheard

    CHORUS

    Voices

Speak for the Unheard Voices

    S   **R**

Hello darling   *Hello darling*

R

She called me darling. Got to love the Brits.

    S   **R**

Are you there?   *Are you there?*

S

What time is it there?
           Why does this boy never know the time difference?

R

It's midnight here.
    Oh shit.

    S

I'm sorry, I hope I didn't wake you.

SPEAKING FOR THE UNHEARD VOICES

R

No, no... I'm up.
Was thinking about you.
Was thinking about what you had said about when you had visited
your high school.
It's not just in the US these horrors are taking place.
We're dealing with a similar monster here in the UK. You recounting
your memories of the high school reminds me of my own childhood.
I think back to being a child and my mother trying to hide us away
from seeing White nationalist marching through otherwise diverse
and peaceful streets. Walking with chained dogs, smashing mailboxes,
and spreading messages of hatred. I think about my mother who
cried due to frustration cause she didn't know how to protect her two
daughters from the evil of this world. Like you I also want to speak for
the unheard.

R
Speak for

S
The Unheard

CHORUS
Speak for the Unheard Voices

R
Open browser
Refresh
Porn...close...close...close... close... close...close...close...
Jesus...
Open new...
Open... Read...
Like...
Open... Read...
What the fuck?!!
Click
Open... Read...
What is happening?
Message

S
I can't sleep.

R
Have you read the news lately?

S
No what happened?

R

Share

S

Click.

Click.

Read.

Pause.

CHORUS

Oh my God.

S

Oh that's horrible.
The police…they…

CHORUS

Click. Click. Click. Click.

R

Left him there… Left that young boy laid under the hot sun for all to see.

S

A black kid.

R

A black youth

S

My heart bleeds.

R

I've been feeling rather hopeless lately.

S

Click

CHORUS

Blood on the ground

S

Hours in the sun.

R

Yellow police tape.

S

Mother screaming
Where is the justice in this world?

SPEAKING FOR THE UNHEARD VOICES

R
What can be done?
I feel so much rage.

> **S**
> What should I do?

> **R**
> What can I do?

> **CHORUS**
What can we do?

> **S**
> He says *I've been feeling rather hopeless lately. This same week... The death of so many black brothers and sisters and then that moment of carrying that noose on my bag through the hallways of my school as a kid. They attack us both physically and mentally. I feel like I need to speak out and I'm growing really tired of feeling like there is nowhere for my voice to be heard. I don't know. That's what I've been wrestling with lately. With so many lives being taken here, it's getting to me. I'm scared to leave the house. Who knows maybe I'll be next.*
> Hello

Silence

> Silence.

> > Hello?

Are you there?
> Hello?

As soon as you get this, message me straight away, let me know you are okay.
> Still haven't heard from you.

Are you alright? Are you okay?
> Silence

Silence
> Silence

> **R**
Speak for

> **S**
> The Unheard

> **CHORUS**
Voices.

S

Speak for

R

The Unheard

CHORUS

Voices

Speak for the Unheard Voices

Speak for the Unheard Voices.

Speak for the Unheard Voices

S

Are you there?

R

I'm here.

S

Where the fuck you been? I've been fucking worrying about you... delete...delete...delete...no actually... Where the fuck did you go? ...delete... Was thinking about you.

R

Was thinking about you too?

Oh I have something to tell you.

S

What?

R

I did it... I caused a fuckin' fire hazard!!! And it was beautiful...

S

Oh shit what did you do?

R

So many people. A Full house of men and women

S

The community

R

Electrifying

S

You actually did it?

R

Standing ovations

SPEAKING FOR THE UNHEARD VOICES

S
They spoke out

R
Unfiltered. Truths

S
You actually did it.

R
Yep. It's time to spread the fire across the pond

S
It's time to join the revolution
After all, like you always say, we are the community's prophet,
politicians and preachers.

R
I hope I'm not being too bold but would you be up for maybe a video chat?

S
Yeah that could be nice.

R
I would love to...get to know you better

———————————

CHORUS

Like
Like
　　　Click
Like
　　　Share
Share
　　　Wait
What?
　　　Comment
Delete
　　　Junk mail
Click
　　　Junk mail
Delete
　　　Open

CHORUS
Speak for the Unheard Voices
Speak for the Unheard Voices.
Speak for the Unheard Voices

The lights shift and focuses on them both.

R
Hey

S
Hey

R
I can't believe I'm actually getting to see your face.

S
Easy now, mister, it's just skype.
How are you doing?

R
I'm great. Got my first hate mail last night.

S
What?

R
Nooses untie from backpack...

S
Dogs and hatemongers fade away...

R
Okay lot more than one. Like a good dozen, it's great.
Graffiti scrubbed away...

S
People standing together

R
United

S
Nooses...

CHORUS
click...

R
Swastikas...

S
click...

R
High school...

SPEAKING FOR THE UNHEARD VOICES

S
chained dogs...

R
broken mail boxes...

S
crooked police...

CHORUS
click, click, click...
Red, white, blue...

S
Red blood on ground,

R
blue sirens, white supremacy...

CHORUS
white bigotry...white privilege...white ignorance...

R
Yellow tape...

S
Mothers screams...

R
black bodies bled...

S
they're hatred...clicks...

R
clicks...

S
clicks...

CHORUS
CLICKS

R
and they have the nerve to say...

S
they have the nerve to claim...

R
        "Oh, you Black Livers, first you take over our
streets, now you're invading our theatres?" yeah...

Then another one just compared me to the Taliban. So I guess
I'm a theatrical terrorist. Like they expect theatre artists to

CHORUS
Sit down, be quiet, not speak

R
to the issues taking place in the world.

S
A terrorist? A terrorist, really?

R
So I'm going to keep at it.
I'm feeling empowered now.

S
I'm feeling empowered now...

CHORUS
We're feeling empowered now.
More than we've ever felt before.
We're going to spread this thing...

S
Fire...

R
City to city

S
Finding artists that have something to say

R
Socially conscious artitsts

S
Artists that want to speak for the Trayvon Martin

CHORUS
Speak for the Unheard Voices
Sandra Bland
Speak for the Unheard Voices
Eric Garner
Speak for the Unheard Voices
Tamir Rice
Speak for the Unheard Voices
Jermaine Carby
Speak for the Unheard Voices
Rekia Boyd

SPEAKING FOR THE UNHEARD VOICES

Speak for the Unheard Voices
Mark Duggan
Speak for the Unheard Voices
Michael Brown
Speak for the Unheard Voices
Speak for the Unheard Voices
Speak for the Unheard Voices
Speak for the Unheard Voices
Speak for the Unheard Voices

End of play.

THE PRINCIPLES OF CARTOGRAPHY

by Winsome Pinnock

CLIFF

Male, black, late twenties/early thirties

ABI

Female black, elderly

CHERRY

Black, late thirties/early forties

CLIFF   Bird in Bush Road, Hereford Retreat, Nutt Street,
Gainer Close, Sumner Road, Daniel Gardens,
/[1]Canaries Close, Jarrett Street, Samuel Street,
Pentridge Street, Cinnamon Close, Finch mews,
Bamber Road, Moody Road, Crane Street,
Diamond Street, Carisbrooke Gardens, Boathouse
Walk

CHERRY   Shoe Zone, Sports Direct, JD Sports.

ABI   Warfarin, Digoxin, Bisoprolol, Donepezil

CHERRY   Angel wants the Jordan Air 4 Retros, but I say the
Converse All Stars are more suitable for school.
He won't have it, pouts his disappointment at me.
Says I want him to look like a fool. So funny.
So sweet. But I can't afford the Jordan Air 4s,
so I buy the Converses and that's the end of it.
He gives me the silent treatment all the way from
Rye Lane to Hanover Park

ABI   When I tell Lola I am three hundred and sixty-two
years old she can't stop giggling. I'm like that fella
on the TV, that doctor whose face regenerates
each decade. Abi, you're too much. She tells me
to stop or she'll split her sides laughing

CLIFF: I cross Roads, Gardens, Closes, and Squares,
scope reality in the names of streets. Embed
them in my mind. I map a walk then, when I'm at
my desk, pin it down with logograms and contour
lines. I retrace my steps, embellish the maps with
flourishes of my own. Carrot symbols mark the
vomit on Pentridge Road, a rose marks the shrine
to a hit-and-run on Rye Lane. My mind, oh my
mind, explodes with images of green and pleasant
lands. I long for open pastures. Concrete kills me.
I'm made of softer climes – the blue spume of the
ocean, particles of sugar and sand

ABI   The communal lounge of the Hanover Park Care
Home is like a waiting room, a processing centre
for people who are refugees from their old lives.
A place of limbo where internally displaced persons
hover between life and death. The highlight of the

---

[1] This speech works like a choral "round". The hyphen marks the point where
Abi and then Cherry join in, each reciting the litany from the beginning.

day is the rattle of Lola's drugs trolley. Sometimes I think it's worse than that filthy hold with its stench of vomit and shit; when we were tortured by the sound of the angry boiling sea and the thump-thump-thump of shark's tails against the stern as they followed us, hungry for a body jumped or thrown overboard

CHERRY   Cheers up when I say we're having McDonald's, though

CLIFF   In the noisy pub a sea of faces: pink, purple, grey. The conversations zip around me. I am invisible. The warm beer leaves a slimy afterthought. I'm the only one who knows that this pub sits on a ley line. I hold the secret to me and remember what the nurse said. Shattered, is what she said. You are shattered. When she says it I see fragments of glass held together for a moment then blast apart in a shower of glistening powder. Between the old life and this one is a gap, like the hole where a tooth should be. My tongue explores it, searching for meaning. Then I'm out on the street again, memorising routes. I look for signs of myself in the street names: King Henry Walk, Miles Chase, Blackboy Lane

CHERRY   We're both hungry and tired. We decide to be kind to each other again. We're not far from the restaurant when all of a sudden – from out of nowhere – four, maybe five, policemen appear

ABI   When we hear the commotion even Lola goes to the window to see what's going on

CHERRY/ABI   A young man. Surrounded by police

CHERRY   It happens every day in London, but it's not the sort of thing you want your kid to see. Four policemen and their prancing dog all over some poor bloke. I should walk away, but I can't. I have to keep watching. I have to bear witness

ABI   They pluck at his shirt, his trousers, turn him around, pluck at his pockets, squeeze his cheeks to look inside his mouth. I recall how they jabbed and prodded us, counted our teeth to determine how healthy we were, before putting us on the block

CHERRY   One of my mates says when they swoop like that it's to intimidate the rest of us, keep us under control

CLIFF   I ain't done nothing. I'm an innocent maker of maps. Ask anybody round here they'll tell you. They've all seen me out and about taking note of the street names. My maps show what the other maps don't tell you. My map marks Mrs Lee's kindness on the corner of Gainer Close, kids' laughter on Sumner Road, the smell of fresh cut grass on Peckham Rye...

ABI   I can't hear what they're saying through the window, but I can tell from the officer's open mouth, his furious frown that they are ordering the man to keep a safe distance. That's when I recognise his face. He is unblemished by time, but I'd recognise his ancient fury anywhere. Lola thinks there is a problem with my memory, but I swear I remember him as if it was yesterday.

CHERRY   The officers stand off as though they're confronted with an angry lion. The man makes them angry and afraid. I will him to do what they tell him to. Don't answer back. Don't make things worse for yourself. He refuses to answer their questions

CLIFF   *(He recites this over and over, getting faster and louder.)* Bird in Bush Road, Hereford Retreat, Nutt Street, Gainer Close, Sumner Road, Daniel Gardens, Samuel Street. Finch Mews, Sumner Road, Diamond Close. Bird in Bush Road, Diamond Close, Cinnamon close, Cinnamon Close Cinnamon Close, Cinnamon Close!

ABI   The officer takes out his Taser, aims it at the man and shoots. Wires whip around his legs. He crumples to the ground.

(Pause.)

CHERRY   Is he dead? Is he dead, Mummy? Mummy, is he dead? This is no place for my boy. I snatch him up and leave. I don't want him to see this. We don't take the bus. I want to walk. We walk past Bird in Bush Road, Hereford Retreat, Nutt Street, Finch Mews, Diamond Close. We walk until I don't know where I am anymore. Me, born and bred here. Me – who knows Peckham like the back of my hand – lost.

ABI   After three hundred years of enduring one indignity after another, I have had enough. As I watch the paralysed boy face down on the ground, I know what I have to do. I have nothing to lose. Lola tries to stop me as I make my way to the reception area, but I am filled with a new energy and she is too heavy-footed to outrun me. In a moment I am out in the open, face to face with the officer. Centuries I've waited to see you again. You and that dog of yours have crossed oceans, deserts, chased me across space and time. Why can't you just let me be? Let the young man go. He has done nothing wrong. The officer's eyes flash with recognition, but he is at pains to pretend that he doesn't know who I am. He ignores me and speaks into his radio. My chest swells with an ancient anger. I snatch the Taser and hold it against his head. Do you know how many times I have dreamed of this, imagined taking your whip out of your hand and letting you have a taste of it? His colleagues stand back. This is not their fight. His forehead is slippery with sweat. He puts his hands up and backs away from me, but I am too quick for him. I aim and fire. Kerchow! The wires shoot straight into his head. As he hits the ground his big purple tongue rolls out of his mouth.

CHERRY   Are we lost, Mum? Something snaps in me. *(Angry.)* For God's sake shut up with your whining. That's right, blame me for everything. I'm sorry I brought you into an imperfect world. Sometimes I wish I'd never given birth to you at all. Well, I'm glad you saw what you did this afternoon. That's right, I'm glad. You're a big boy now. It's time you learned what's in store for you. And he's sobbing with a new unwanted wisdom. He's crying like he'll never stop. I scoop him into my arms. I fold him into me, my love a force field around him. I hold onto him tight tight tight. My precious, my beautiful boy. I hug him until we both return to ourselves.

ABI   But of course all I do is watch helplessly through the window as the officer cuffs the young man's hands behind his back and the paramedics load him into the ambulance. Lola says that's enough excitement for the day, and gives me a cup of water to wash down the tablets

CHERRY   I love the night time when my boy sleeps. When he draws even breaths and his face settles into its serene beauty. Then I'm free to roam. Two clicks of a mouse and I'm talking to a faceless wonder in another world. Not tonight. Tonight I search for another excitement. I find it soon enough: What we saw recorded on a smart phone behind net curtains. It don't look the way I remember it – the colours less sharply defined, the emotions fuzzy. Freeze the frame, zoom in on my Angel. His hand in mine, his mouth stretched across his teeth, his cheeks bunched up and distorted, making him look like an octogenarian. Twenty years between him and the young man, yet the puzzlement and fear on their faces make them indistinguishable. When I hear movement in his room I go to find him propped against pillows, holding a pencil, his face creased in concentration as he scratches at a piece of paper. What are you doing? Why aren't you asleep? "I've made you a map Mum," He's drawn our route in meticulous detail. At the location of the scene he's drawn where the man fell, the placement of the police, but he's rubbed them out again. All that's left of them are faint lines and eraser fluff. The rest of our route that day intact. He gives me the map and says "Now you'll never be lost again,"

CLIFF   The electricity, when it shoots through me, illuminates neural pathways. I shine so bright they don't dare touch me. They let me go. I'm Frankenstein's monster with heightened senses: I smell and taste the sweetness of Cinnamon Close, the rocks on the buildings glisten on Diamond Close, Blake's angels sing in the trees on Bird in Bush road; the pavement cracks and is riven in two, fills with an expanse of water on Boathouse walk. My mind takes an aerial view. The map lights a path: I make my way home.

CLIFF   Bird in Bush Road, Hereford Retreat, Nutt Street, Gainer Close, Sumner Road, Daniel Gardens, /[2]Canaries Close, Jarrett Street, Samuel Street, Pentridge Street, Cinnamon Close, Finch mews, Bamber Road, Moody Road, Crane Street, Diamond Street, Carisbrooke Gardens, Boathouse Walk

The lights go down as they continue to recite.

---

[2] This is a repetition of the choral round from the top of the scene.

LEFT HANGIN'

by Trish Cooke

CELIA

(Kane's Mother) 40-year-old black woman
educated working class

KANE

(Celia's Son) 23-year-old black man
looks street-wise but is autistic

SARAH

(Kane's Girlfriend) 23-year-old white woman
pretty, fashion conscious

ZEB

(Kane's Friend) 23-year-old mixed race man
wide boy

MICK

(Sara's Father) 45-year-old white man
tough British gangster type

POLICE MAN

White

OFFICIAL

Announcer of newspaper articles, statistics and facts

SCENE ONE

On a screen we see the Guardian headline **'Deaths in police custody at highest level for five years'** *dated 23rd July 2015. On the screen in bold letters it says:*

'The latest official statistics show that in 2013-14, 68 people took their own lives within two days of being arrested or detained, the highest figure for a decade.'

Below the screen, in a half light, stands CELIA, a forty-year-old black woman with a vacant look on her face.

CELIA

They told me he hung himself... But I know my son. *(Beat.)* When he started going out with Sarah,

A pretty white girl, SARAH, steps forward.

CELIA

I warned him. Told him white girls are different. Any sign of trouble and it would be

SARAH

(Mid argument.) Fuck off, you black bastard

CELIA

And before he knew it she'd have the old bill round and he wouldn't stand a chance. But he didn't want to know...

A young black man, KANE, steps forward.

KANE

You don't understand, Ma. We love each other

CELIA

(Shrugs.) I couldn't force him to listen. I had no right to break his dream.

KANE kisses CELIA on the cheek. She does not react straight away. Instead she touches her cheek moments later as if he's not there.

On the screen is 'the safeguarding adults practitioner guide 2013' for central london community healthcare. An OFFICIAL steps forward.

OFFICIAL

The UK legal definition, as directed by the Lord Chancellor's department, of a vulnerable adult is: 'A person who is or may be in need of community services by reason of disability, age or illness: and is or may be unable to take care of or unable to protect himself against significant harm or exploitation.'

LEFT HANGIN'

CELIA
When he was sixteen months old Kane was identified by health professionals as having behaviours that are consistent with a person suffering from Autism.

KANE
(Reciting like a shopping list.) Poor attention span, hyperactivity, dyslexia and difficulty managing emotional relationships.

CELIA
Then there was the ADHD. From the age of five and up to his death Kane had the involvement of specialist consultants, education psychologists, local social services department and mental health specialists.

KANE
I just want to be 'normal' like everyone else.

CELIA
He had difficulty in being able to successfully manage friendships or relationships with appropriate individuals so instead he made friends with other delinquent juveniles.

KANE
They accept me as I am…

CELIA
He was easily manipulated, influenced, bullied, teased and they often made him a source of their own entertainment.

KANE
It's okay. They're just having a laugh, Mum.

CELIA
Between the ages of eleven and eighteen Kane became heavily involved in crime.

On the screen – BBC News UK – 23rd July 2015 – the headline is: **'Custody deaths represent failure' – Theresa May.** *In bold letters it says:*

> 'The Independent Police Complaints Commission
> says there were 17 deaths in or following police custody
> in 2014-15. That figure was at its highest at 36 in 2004-5'

CELIA
Yes, I know he wasn't easy. He got up to all kinds of things. But kill himself? No. It doesn't…it doesn't make sense. I know my son.

Lights change.

SCENE TWO

KANE and SARAH hold hands. They look lovingly into each other's eyes.

CELIA
Kane met Sarah when he was sixteen. At the time she had been
experiencing relationship problems with her father and she had
left the family home to stay with Kane who had moved in with his
grandfather. I can't say I was happy about it. See, he had met Sarah
through her older sister Yvette. Yvette was working at the Young
Offenders Institution Kane had been attending. Kane had told me
that Yvette (Sarah's sister) was in a relationship with a person she
had met in the institution. I was not impressed with the disregard for
the rules and boundaries for personal relationships with inmates.
I didn't approve of how Yvette conducted herself and knew from
what Kane had told me that Sarah was easily influenced by her big
sister. I knew immediately these were not the kind of people that
Kane should be associating himself with. When things looked like
they might be getting serious I remember sitting Sarah down and
telling her

CELIA
(To SARAH.) He's not normal… Kane might present himself as a
smart and intelligent individual but he's got a number of complex
issues. He's emotionally sensitive about the things he cares about.
You mustn't play with his emotions or take advantage of him.

KANE
Sarah's not like that, Mum.

CELIA
I asked her if she understood what I was saying, she said

SARAH
(In love.) Yeah. I just want to be with Kane…

MICK, (a sinister looking gangster type) SARAH's dad steps forward.

MICK
(To KANE.) You better watch your step with my daughter, lad. I've got
my eye on you.

CELIA
Kane told me Sarah's parents weren't happy with them seeing each
other because in their eyes Kane was a prolific offender, just like
Sarah's dad had been when he was younger, and they didn't want
that for their daughter. Kane and Sarah didn't listen to any of us.
(Beat.) Then Sarah got pregnant…

MICK *(To SARAH.)*
You're not having it! End of!

SARAH
But Dad!

MICK *(To SARAH.)*
You're sixteen years old! You've got your whole life ahead of you!

CELIA
It broke Kane's heart when Sarah had the termination.

KANE
Like nobody even cares what I want...

CELIA
A few months later though...

SARAH
(Happy excited.) I'm pregnant!

CELIA
He was excited. He liked children. Children didn't judge him.
He couldn't wait for the baby to be born. He and Sarah moved into
a flat, that Sarah's mother had put the bond down on. The flat was
in Sarah's name. They went through the whole pregnancy. The
whole nine months. And then Harvey Lee was born.

KANE
Asleep.

CELIA
Kane struggled to understand that Harvey had died and that he
had had no control over the outcome. He found the delivery and
the aftermath hard to deal with. He couldn't support himself never
mind a grieving mother and Sarah needed him to be there for her
desperately but he just couldn't cope. I encouraged Sarah to go
and stay at her parents so she could get the support she needed
but she wouldn't listen. She insisted she wanted to stay with Kane,
even though it was clear he wasn't able to give her the support she
needed. I was worried for him. For them. The cracks were beginning
to show in their relationship.

It was around this time I noticed the level of demands Sarah would
make on Kane and I knew that this was not a relationship that Kane
was going to be able to cope with emotionally or psychologically.
I noticed she would hit, nip or kick him on the sly and when he
reacted she would behave as if she hadn't done anything. I know
because I saw her do it and he just took it.

KANE

It's okay, Ma. We're gonna try for another baby...

CELIA

I explained that I was concerned about them trying for another baby. I was worried about his mental health and the damage losing another child might do to him. I told them even if the baby lived that they wouldn't have an easy time.

KANE

Sarah won't let me talk about Harvey Lee anymore and I miss him. Every time I bring him up she tells me she doesn't want to talk about him... But she wants another baby...and she wants me to make her pregnant. She goes on about it all day, every single day. Sometimes I leave the flat for days just to get away from the noise.

CELIA

A few months later Sarah became pregnant again, her third pregnancy. I was scared that the baby might not make it and if it did, I was afraid she might play games with Kane's head and use the child to manipulate him emotionally. I wasn't happy but what could I do? Kane became very detached from the pregnancy.

KANE

I tried not to think about it but I couldn't help it. I came up with names... Delicia Ann if it was a girl and Ashley Ryan if it was a boy. Sarah had chosen the name Harvey Lee so she said I could choose this one. I was scared. Nervous. Frightened the same thing would happen again. Maybe I was being punished for something. Maybe I wasn't good enough, I dunno. I just couldn't bond with the baby inside of Sarah, not this time. Not yet.

CELIA

The place they were living in didn't have sufficient heating so I helped them get another place. I paid the deposit and initial rent. This time the flat was in both their names, though Sarah's mum wasn't happy about this. She wanted the flat to be in her daughter's name only, in case anything was to happen between them, then at least her daughter would have a home. To me it felt like plans were already being made... Like Sarah was preparing to leave him. I was anxious for my son. *(Beat.)* Precisely forty weeks after the birth of Harvey Lee, Emma Yvette was born. Five weeks early.

KANE and SARAH dote over the new baby.

CELIA

(To KANE.) I asked what happened to the name he chose

LEFT HANGIN'

KANE

I know Ma, I wanted Delicia Ann but I let her choose the name cos
I don't want to argue with her in case she takes the baby away...

CELIA

Once Emma was born I noticed a significant change in the tone of the
conversations I would have with Kane.

KANE

There are just so many things to buy. And no matter what I give Sarah,
it's never enough. She tells me if I don't get stuff for them
I'll never see Emma again.

CELIA

He said that Sarah was threatening to get social services to stop him
from seeing Emma and she was going to use his disabilities and mental
health issues against him. He was ashamed of his condition. Thought
he would not be perceived as a good father because of his autism.
(Beat.) He did what he had to do, to provide for Sarah and Emma.

KANE

Sometimes that meant breaking the law.

SARAH

(To KANE, mid argument.) I can do anything I want and there's nothing
you can do about it!

KANE

You're just as guilty as me! You spend the money!

SARAH

Who's going to believe *you*?
You're the one with a criminal record! Everything we've done illegally
is done in your name so there's no trace back to me!

KANE

What about all the bank transfers? All the money I put into your account?

SARAH

I just tell them I don't know where you got the money from. Nothing to
do with me!

KANE

Anytime we have an argument she goes to her mum and dad's and
tells them I'm no good. She takes Emma and sometimes stays there
for weeks. Whenever I arrange to bring Emma to see my side of the
family, she takes her to her parents'. I let Mum think I'm just not
turning up but it's Sarah... She won't let me... She says she'll take
Emma away for good if I don't do as she says. I don't tell anyone.
My friends would only laugh at me... I'm ashamed...

CELIA

I worked out what Sarah was doing. I told Kane that this was not okay and that it was a form of mental abuse and that Sarah was seeking to exploit his worst fear and using it to her advantage. She knew about his psychological and emotional issues and she was using them against him. I told him that he didn't have to put up with it and we could help him.

KANE

No Mum, don't do anything! I just want to see Emma. As long as I see Emma every day, I'm okay.

CELIA

One evening he called me, in tears.

KANE

(Crying hysterically.) I have to get a job. Sarah and her mum have been at me to find work... Mum what am I going to do? Sarah's mum has told her to leave me if I can't find a job. She says I'm a waste of space who doesn't deserve to have Sarah or Emma.

CELIA

(Trying to reassure him.) It's okay... Don't worry. I know it's not going to be easy but if you try really hard you'll find a job and then Sarah's mum might ease up on you.

CELIA

Over the next two years Kane did his best to get work. He started doing temporary work and it really helped him. He was able to escape the abuse he was experiencing in the home. He liked working and the agency work allowed him to go to different places for short periods of time which he was able to manage. He sometimes did sixty hour weeks to get out of the house and to make money to give to Sarah for her and Emma. He was providing for his family, legally and he was happy. It's the best I've ever seen him... (Beat.) That's why it doesn't add up... What they said he did. It doesn't make sense... None of it. He has... He *had* a way of doing things. Maybe due to his autism or his ADHD, I don't know. I knew his pattern. If ever he had a problem, he would call me and if he didn't get through right away, he would call again and again and keep calling until he got through but that night he...he never called. Not once.

SCENE THREE

A young mixed race man, ZEB, steps forward.

ZEB

(Uneasy.) I... I got a text from him.

LEFT HANGIN'

CELIA
When his friend, Zeb, showed me the text, I knew it wasn't from Kane. Kane doesn't write like that. It's not his style. The words were written out in full and in grammatically correct sentences. I always had a joke with him about his text spelling and shortening of words

KANE
You don't get it Ma. That's how we text.

CELIA
It would irritate me cos I knew he was smart and writing words wrong when you knew better was another way of selling yourself short to fit the stereotype that society wants you to be, in my eyes. And my boy knew better. I always told him 'Be all that you are. Be smart.'

A POLICE MAN steps forward.

POLICE
It's an open and shut case. There is no reason to believe it is anything other than a suicide.

CELIA
No. I know he was into things he shouldn't have been into. Moved with people he shouldn't have. Got himself involved in business he had no business getting involved in... But he was making a change.

An irate SARAH lashes out at KANE.

SARAH
You dare, you fuckin' black bastard!

CELIA
I heard they'd had a fight...some argument...he and Sarah... Kane was in receipt of high level living allowance from the age of twelve to seventeen and he had made a recent adult claim for personal independence payments. He was successful in obtaining the benefit award. Sarah was the carer in the personal independence award. Kane told me he wasn't keen on claiming. He said that once his childhood claim had stopped he hadn't bothered to make a claim as an adult for fear of how he would be perceived as a father by his daughter. But Sarah had been insistent on pressing him to apply for the additional money so she could buy more stuff for her and Emma. They'd been arguing about this. Kane had come in after a night out and Sarah was on his case.

SARAH
Go on, hit me! Hit me!

ZEB
Come on mate, out of 'ere. Walk. She's goading yer.

KANE

(To SARAH.) Stop it man! You're winding me up! You're just winding me up!

ZEB

Take her for a walk. (To EMMA.) Get your coat Emma.

KANE

(To EMMA.) Wanna go for a walk with Daddy? Let's go get sweeties.

CELIA

Zeb said Kane did the right thing, he walked away.

ZEB

Twenty minutes later, I sent a text to Kane, telling him to get back to the flat cos things were kicking off. Sarah had called Five-O. Said Kane had run off with their kid.

CELIA

What I don't get is how a six foot man can hang himself in a six foot two door frame. I know it's possible cos that's what they say happened but when I run through the motions every day and see him fastening and tying the knot. Putting his head in the noose. Lifting up his knees so his feet don't touch the ground and holding on until the knot tightens around his neck. Surely when it hurt, when the tug of the rope pulled on his neck, surely then he would have allowed his legs to drop down to scrape his toes across the floor. Surely he would have just stood up. Took his head out. Walked away.

The POLICE MAN is trying to calm KANE down.

POLICE

Come on son, quietly does it. There's reason to believe there's been a disturbance here and we need you to leave the premises.

KANE

(Angry and upset.) I haven't done anything. What are you accusing me of? I haven't done anything!

POLICE

The lady says she feels threatened by your behaviour and so we have to ask you to leave.

KANE

This is my flat. I don't have to go. I haven't done anything.

POLICE

Come on lad, hand the kid over and calm down. Your kid's getting upset.

KANE

(Getting irate.) I'm not going anywhere. I haven't done anything *(Hysterical.)* Gerroff me! Leave me alone! Let me go!

CELIA

I know what you're thinking…he's just another statistic and I'm just another black grieving mother who can't…who won't accept that her son has gone but that's not how it is. Even the Coroner held back the body. Even he thought more questions needed to be asked.

SCENE FOUR

A hysterical KANE is in a police cell.

POLICE

Okay son…calm down.

KANE

(Upset.) But I didn't do anything! Why am I here? I didn't do anything! I'm not well! I'm not well!

POLICE

Are you on any form of medication?

KANE

No…yes… I… I have ADHD. I started some new pills last week but they're no good. They send my head off so I stopped taking 'em.

POLICE

(To another officer.) Get the girl to bring them in.

KANE

They don't agree with me.

POLICE

No worries. We'll sort something.

CELIA

The ADHD diagnosis and medication history is present on the police database. So many unanswered questions… Like did the custody officers booking Kane in make a note of his ADHD diagnosis? Was a police doctor contacted in regards to the medication? Did the police doctor have specialist training and knowledge to deal with detainees with conditions such as Kane's? Did they know he had been drinking? Did the medical assessment of Kane include a blood screen for skunk weed or cocaine? If skunk weed and/or cocaine was present in his system would the police doctor or any other health professional give authorisation for Kane to have any prescribed medication such as Concerta XL? Why weren't the mental health professionals alerted?

On the screen – BBC News UK – 23rd July 2015 headline –

'Each death in police custody represents a failure and can "dramatically" undermine relations between the public and police, says the home secretary.'

OFFICIAL

The Independent Police Complaints Commission chairwoman, Dame Anne Owers, said the custody system suffered from 'inadequate risk assessments, token checks on a person in custody, insufficient handovers between custody staff, a failure to recognise or properly deal with people with mental health concerns or substance abuse issues, poor liaison between police and other agencies'.

The POLICE MAN give KANE the pills.

We hear birds singing.

KANE

I must have zonked out. Morning came. I felt groggy. They gave me my things and I headed home.*(Beat.)* When I got to my flat, it was empty. Everything gone. My Emma. My little girl, gone. It was too much... I couldn't think straight...

From behind, KANE is grabbed by the throat.

MICK

Fuck with my daughter eh? You black bastard! You lay a finger on her and I'll kill you, didn't I tell you!

KANE

(To MICK.) But I never touched her, I swear!

MICK

That's not what she said!

KANE

She's a liar! Ask Zeb! He was there!

KANE

I could see daylight coming in and out – some bright light shit burning my eyes and my heart was pumping like the whole of me was a great big giant heart beat. Could feel fingers digging into my skin. Could feel my body leaving the ground but I couldn't fight them off. Couldn't focus. Like I was wading through fog, quick sand, everything was slowing down. Then there was something around my neck, rough rope. They had my hands held tight behind my back and were holding my knees up. I was gagging and they wouldn't ease up. Could feel the rope getting tighter around my neck. Could hear them rushing off. Could hear their car drive away. And in that moment I thought... Kane...man get it together else you're dead.

LEFT HANGIN'

A moment. Lights dim.

CELIA
(Beat.) So, what am I supposed to do with all these thoughts going round in my head? Will I ever know what actually happened…?
All I want is a proper investigation… Is that too much to ask?

On the screen – BBC News UK – 23rd July 2015 headline –

**Theresa May to launch independent review
of deaths in police custody**

OFFICIAL
(Voice over.) An independent review of police custody deaths in England and Wales has been announced by the home secretary. The review is expected to cover the lead-up to deaths, the immediate aftermath and how families are helped or supported during official investigations. It will assess whether police officers properly understand mental health issues, the availability of appropriate healthcare, the use of restraint techniques, and suicides in the first 48 hours of detention.

Blackout.

THE INTERROGATION OF SANDRA BLAND

Transcript and stage concept by Mojisola Adebayo

Dedicated to Sandra Bland (1987-2015) and all black people in the USA and Britain who have died in police custody.

In June 2016 Artistic Directors of the Future (ADF) invited me and several other black playwrights to write a fifteen minute play for the first 'Black Lives, Black Words' event in London, at Bush Theatre. The brief was to respond to the question, 'do black lives matter today?' I felt both overwhelmed and humbled at the gravity of the task. I had no idea where to begin. Then I remembered Sandra Bland, having followed (like so many of us have done) an appalling online trail of humiliations and violations of our African kin, across the Atlantic and on our own European island, Britain. I remembered how awed I was by Sandra Bland during the roadside interrogation that lead to her brutal arrest and eventual death by hanging in police custody, recorded on the dashboard camera of the police car that pulled her over. I was moved by Sandra Bland's courage, her wit, intelligence, integrity, strength, tenacity and helplessness in the face of the arresting police officer. The interrogation also struck me as a horribly gripping and dramatic 'scene' that escalates with devastating dramaturgical effect. I thought, I could not write anything more compelling or important than this. I could not write anything that demonstrates more acutely the various levels of anti-black racism and white supremacist mentality in action, than this. However, I did not want to just re-stage the real life scene. Anyone can click on 'youtube' to see it. I have no taste for verbatim plays that only translate reality rather than transport the audience imaginatively. I want theatre to do something that a webpage, a news clip or a mainstream documentary cannot do. Then an idea came to me. Let us take the words of Sandra Bland and have them spoken by 100 black women who all play her. Sandra Bland was evidently a brilliant woman; she was sharp, clever, funny, brave, dignified, talented and educated. There was no one like her and her life can never be replaced. Yet any one of us black women could have been in Sandra Bland's shoes. My idea in having Sandra Bland played by a huge chorus of black women is that she is shown as an everyblackwoman. We elevate Sandra Bland's status and the status of all black people who have faced similar situations, through the amplification of the voice, a magnification of the struggle. The performance is in this way a theatrical memorial to Sandra Bland and whom she represents. This is a spoken requiem. Furthermore, by magnifying and illuminating the encounter, audiences are encouraged to investigate the scene and interrogate the interrogation. Lastly, in this performance I want to offer an opportunity for a civic ritual through which as many of us as possible can creatively participate in the movement, Black Lives Matter. So I sat down at my desk, watched the online clip over and again and transcribed the roadside interrogation and arrest of Sandra Bland by State Trooper Brian Encinia on the 10 July 2015, in Waller County, Texas, USA. Below is that transcription.

THE INTERROGATION OF SANDRA BLAND

We chose not to stage the piece as planned in 2016 as the legal proceedings were still in process. Moreover, I really wanted Sandra Bland's family to give us their blessing for the performance to go ahead. We tried but ADF were not able to reach the family. This raises a question about the ethics of going ahead with the staging. For me this question was answered by the fact that Sandra Bland was herself an active part of the Black Lives Matter movement. Importantly, Bland specifically called to a passer by filming her arrest, 'thank you for recording! Thank you'. Lastly, the dashcam recording is already in the public domain. I hope that, as we approach the first staging of The Interrogation of Sandra Bland, at Bush Theatre on 24 March 2017, we have, in some way, her own spiritual and political blessing for her unaltered recorded words to be heard and multiplied, loud and clear, with full emotional commitment, in the theatre. If it was me, I would want people to know what happened and how. This is another way of recording and hopefully making something beautiful out of the brutal, something revolutionary out of the revolting abuse of life. Sandra Bland was arrested when she was on her own and she died alone in a police cell. The amplification of her voice in the staging becomes a collective gesture of solidarity and support. Her voice will not be alone in this moment. Therefore, dear Sandra Bland, wherever your spirit rests or soars, this performance is dedicated to you. May it honour you and show you the respect you deserve. It is dedicated furthermore to all black people who have died in police custody in the USA and Britain. With thanks to Simeilia Hodge-Dallaway and Elayce Ismail who originally helped to develop this project, Black Lives Matter, Black Lives, Black Words, everyone at Bush Theatre, London and all the women who perform in this project. Our deep condolences go to all of Sandra Bland's family and friends. Thank you for recording. Thank you to everyone involved.

I now offer some further staging notes, arising from my vision for the piece, illustrated above. I have not prescribed how the lines should shared by multiple voices because it is important that this publication in itself stands as a true recording of the encounter at the roadside. Furthermore, it is important that forthcoming directors experiment and feel creatively free in rehearsals to find what feels right. I do not know yet what it will look like or sound like on stage. The transcript and these notes are a map, not the destination. However, it is crucial that Sandra Bland is played and her words are spoken by a large cast of 100 black female actors. If this is not logistically possible, this could alternatively comprise of a core group of around 10 black female actors who rehearse professionally and are then joined in rehearsals by a large community chorus of culturally diverse women for shorter periods of rehearsal. As directed, some lines can be spoken collectively en mass, some lines can be taken by one woman, some in pairs, groups and so on. This is for the director to work out with the actors. I suggest paying attention to Sandra Bland's own striking use of repetition. Where a line is repeated it could be interesting to have several voices repeat. The lines and meanings should flow. This is like playing music through words, you have to feel it, you have to listen, deeply. The audience too should feel like participants, not mere witnesses and this sense can guide the quality of playing. Whatever you do, this piece cannot be reduced to a naturalistic staging by three people behind a fourth wall, that would miss the point entirely. Sandra Bland must be amplified, elevated and magnified, for the reasons I discuss above. There is power in collective artistic activism. The words of Encinia however, are to be spoken by one solitary white male actor, present on stage. There is also a brief exchange with an unnamed white female police officer, which should be played by just one white female actor, also physically present. The white police officers must be part of the stage picture. In terms of playing style, this is a study, an interrogation of an interrogation. As such the text should be spoken with absolute clarity and precision, observing punctuation including exclamation and question marks. The audience must not lose a word unless it is deliberately inaudible. However, there is no need for emotional detachment, everyone is playing a person, you cannot act a symbol or a function, this is not reading the news, work out what is happening emotionally to the characters and commit to it. It is not, in my opinion, necessary to use North American accents, unless it feels right to the actor themselves. What is more important is a sense of the African Diasporic rhythm and tone that Sandra Bland displays, black musicality in speech, whether this has African-American, Caribbean, African or black British flavours, to me this does not matter. It is important to the inclusive ethic of the work that people who are D/deaf or hearing impaired are not excluded from the performance, as performers and spectators. Therefore integration of sign languages, and or surtitles, is encouraged. The use of / in a line indicates where the next speaking actor should inter-cut with their line and dialogue overlaps. Pauses should be observed. It might be of interest to explore stylized movement at points and the use and exchange of looks could be key, but whatever movement there is, like all of the staging, it should be kept extremely simple and clear. Let the words do the work.

TRANSCRIPTION

ENCINIA Hello ma'am.

BLAND Hi...

ENCINIA We're the Texas Highway Patrol and the reason for your stop is because you didn't...you failed to signal the lane change. You got your driver's license and registration with you? What's wrong?

BLAND *(Faintly.)* Nothing's wrong.

(Long pause as he looks at the documents.)

ENCINIA How long have you been in Texas?

BLAND Just got here yesterday.

ENCINIA Okay. *(Pause.)* Do you have a driver's license?

BLAND Didn't I give you my driver's license?

ENCINIA No ma'am. *(BLAND inaudible.)* Okay. *(Pause.)* Okay. Where you headed to now?

(BLAND says something casual but inaudible.)

ENCINIA Okay. You give me a few minutes all right?

BLAND All right.

(Long pause as ENCINIA returns. Then approaches BLAND again.)

ENCINIA Okay, ma'am. *(Pause.)* You okay?

BLAND I'm waiting on you, you... This is your job. I'm waiting on you. When're you going / to let me go?

ENCINIA I don't know, you seem very irritated.

BLAND I am. I really am. Cause I feel like it's crap what I'm getting a ticket for. I was getting out of your way. You were speeding up, tailing me, so I move over and you stop me.
So yeah, I am a little irritated, but that doesn't stop you from giving me a ticket, so *(inaudible)* ticket.

ENCINIA Are you done?

BLAND You asked me what was wrong and I told you.

ENCINIA Okay.

BLAND So now I'm done, yeah.

ENCINIA Okay. You mind putting out your cigarette, please? If you don't mind?

BLAND I'm in my car why do I have to put out my cigarette?

ENCINIA Well you can step on out now.

BLAND I don't have to step out of my car.

ENCINIA Step out of the car.

BLAND Why am I...

ENCINIA Step out of the car!

BLAND No, no, you don't have the right.

ENCINIA Step / out of the car!

BLAND You do not have the right to do that...

ENCINIA I do have the right now step out / or I will remove you.

BLAND I refuse to say, I refuse to talk to you other than to identify myself / I am getting removed for a failure to signal?

ENCINIA Step out or I will remove you. I'm giving you a lawful order. Get out of the car now, or I'm gonna remove you.

BLAND And I'm calling my lawyer.

ENCINIA I'm going to yank you out of here. *(Reaches inside the car.)*

BLAND Okay, you're going to yank me out of my car?

ENCINIA Get out.

BLAND Okay, alright.

ENCINIA *(Calling in backup.)* 25-47.

BLAND Let's do this.

ENCINIA Yeah, we're going to. *(Grabs for BLAND.)*

BLAND Don't touch me!

ENCINIA Get out of the car!

BLAND Don't touch me. Don't touch me! I'm not under arrest – you don't have the right to / take me out of the car.

ENCINIA You are under arrest!

BLAND I'm under arrest? / For what? For what? For what?

THE INTERROGATION OF SANDRA BLAND

ENCINIA *(To dispatch.)* 25-47 county fm 10-98 *(inaudible)* send me another unit. *(To BLAND.)* Get out of the car! Get out of the car – now!

BLAND Why am I being apprehended? You're trying to give me a ticket / for failure…

ENCINIA I said get out of the car!

BLAND Why am I being apprehended? / You just opened my car door, you just opened my car door…

ENCINIA I'm giving you a lawful order. I'm going to drag you out of here.

BLAND So you're gon, you're threatening to drag me out of my own car?

ENCINIA GET OUT OF THE CAR!

BLAND And then you're gonna / stun me?

ENCINIA I WILL LIGHT YOU UP! GET OUT!

BLAND Wow.

ENCINIA NOW! *(Draws stun gun and points it at BLAND.)*

BLAND Wow. Wow. *(BLAND exits car.)*

ENCINIA Get out of the car!

BLAND For a failure to signal? You're doing all of this / for a failure to signal?

ENCINIA Get over there.

BLAND Right. Yeah, yeah, let's take this to court / let's do this.

ENCINIA Go ahead.

BLAND For a failure to signal? Yep, for a failure to signal!

ENCINIA Get off the phone! / Get off the phone!

BLAND I'm not on the phone. / I have a right to record. This is my property. This is my property.

ENCINIA Put your phone down. Put your phone down!

BLAND Sir?

ENCINIA Put your phone down, right now! Put your phone down!

(BLAND slams phone down on her trunk.)

BLAND For a fucking failure to signal. My goodness. / Y'all are interesting. Very interesting.

ENCINIA Come over here. Come over here now.

BLAND You feelin' good about yourself?

ENCINIA Stand right here. / Stand right there.

BLAND You feelin' good about yourself? For a failure to signal? / You feel real good about yourself don't you? / You feel good about yourself don't you?

ENCINIA Turn around. Turn around. Turn around now. / Put your hands behind your back and turn around.

BLAND What, what, why am I being arrested?

ENCINIA Turn around…

BLAND Why can't you… Can you tell me why…

ENCINIA I'm giving you a lawful order. I will tell you.

BLAND Why am I being arrested?

ENCINIA Turn around!

BLAND Why won't you tell me that part?

ENCINIA I'm giving you a lawful order. Turn around…

BLAND Why will you not tell me / what's going on?

ENCINIA You are not complying.

BLAND I'm not complying 'cause you just pulled me out of my car!

ENCINIA TURN AROUND!

BLAND Are you fucking kidding me? This is some bull… / You know it is!

ENCINIA Put your hands behind your back.

BLAND 'Cause you know this straight bullshit. And you're full of shit! Full of straight shit! That's all y'all are is some straight scaredy fucking cops. South Carolina got y'all bitch asses scared. That's all it is. Fucking scared of a female.

ENCINIA If you would've just listened.

BLAND I was trying to sign the fucking ticket – whatever.

ENCINIA Stop moving!

BLAND Are you fucking serious?

ENCINIA Stop moving!

THE INTERROGATION OF SANDRA BLAND

BLAND Oh I can't wait 'til we go to court. Ooh I can't wait. I cannot wait 'til we go to court. I can't waaait! Ooh I can't wait! You want me to sit down now?

ENCINIA No.

BLAND Or are you going to throw me to the floor? That would make you feel better about yourself?

ENCINIA Knock it off!

BLAND Nah that would make you feel better about yourself? That would make you feel real good wouldn't it? Pussy ass. Fucking pussy. For a failure to signal you're doing all of this. In little ass Praire View, Texas. My God they, they must have…

ENCINIA You were getting a warning, until now you're going to jail.

BLAND I'm getting a – for what? / For what?

ENCINIA You can come read.

BLAND I'm getting a warning for what? For what!?

ENCINIA Stay right here.

BLAND Well you just pointed me over there!

ENCINIA I said stay right there.

BLAND Get your fucking mind right. Ooh I swear on my life, y'all are some pussies. A pussy-ass cop, for a fucking signal / you're gonna take me to jail. What a pussy! What a pussy… What a p–

ENCINIA *(Either to dispatch, or the officer arriving on scene.)* I got her in control she's in some handcuffs.

BLAND You're about to break my fucking wrist!

ENCINIA Stop moving.

BLAND I'm standing still! You keep moving me, goddammit!

ENCINIA Stay right here. Stand right there.

BLAND Don't touch me. Fucking pussy – for a traffic ticket. Doing all this bullshit…for a traffic ticket… *(Short pause then door slams.)*

ENCINIA Come read right over here. This right here says 'a warning.' You started creating the problems.

BLAND You asked me what was wrong! / I'm trying to tell you –

ENCINIA Do you have anything on your person that's illegal?

BLAND Do I feel like I have anything on me? This a fucking maxi dress.

ENCINIA I'm gonna remove your, I'm gonna remove your glasses.

BLAND This a maxi dress. *(Inaudible.)*

ENCINIA Come on over here.

BLAND Fucking assholes. For a – you about to break my wrist. Can you stop?! You're about to fucking break my wrist! *(Screaming.)* STOOOOOP!!!

ENCINIA Stop moving! Stop now! Stop it!

(BLAND squeals.)

FEMALE OFFICER: Stop resisting ma'am.

ENCINIA If you would stop then I would tell you!

BLAND *(Crying.)* For a fucking traffic ticket...

ENCINIA Now stop!

BLAND *(Crying.)* You are such a pussy. You are such a pussy.

FEMALE OFFICER: No, you are! / You should not be fighting.

BLAND *(Crying.)* For a fucking traffic signal! / For a traffic signal. For a traffic signal.

ENCINIA You are yanking around, when you pull away from me / you're resisting arrest.

BLAND *(Crying.)* This make you feel real good don't it. It make you feel real good don't it? A female for a traffic ticket, for a traffic ticket. / Don't it make you feel good Officer Encinia? I know it make you feel real good. You're a real man now. You just slammed me, knocked my head into the ground. I got epilepsy, you motherfucker!

FEMALE OFFICER: *(Faintly.)* I got it. I got it. *(To ENCINIA.)* Take care of yourself.

ENCINIA Good. Good.

BLAND Good? / Good?!

FEMALE OFFICER: / You should have thought about it before you started resisting.

BLAND All right, all right this is real good. Real good for a female, yeah. Y'all strong. / Y'all real strong.

ENCINIA I want you to wait right here. Wait right here.

THE INTERROGATION OF SANDRA BLAND

BLAND I can't go anywhere with your fucking knee in my back, duh!

ENCINIA I'm gon open your door.

FEMALE POLICE OFFICER: Okay.

ENCINIA *(Pause then to a bystander.)* You need to leave!
You need to leave! You need to leave!

(Time passes. Bland continues to cry, repeating, "for a traffic signal, full of shit, really? Really for a traffic signal??" etc, but much of it is inaudible.)

ENCINIA For a warning, for a warning you're going to jail…

BLAND Whatever / whatever, whatever…

ENCINIA for resisting arrest. Stand up.

BLAND If I could / I can't.

ENCINIA Okay, roll over.

BLAND I can't even fucking feel my arms!

ENCINIA Tuck your knee in, tuck your knee in.

BLAND *(Crying.)* Goddamn. I can't *(Muffled.)*

ENCINIA Listen, listen: you're going to sit up on your butt.

BLAND *(Crying.)* You just slammed my head into the ground and /
you do not even care about that. I can't even hear!

(Simultaneously.) **ENCINIA** Sit up on your butt. **FEMALE
OFFICER** Listen to how he is telling you to get up. Yes you can.

BLAND *(Crying.)* He slammed my fucking head into the ground.

ENCINIA Sit up on your butt. Sit up on your butt.

BLAND *(Crying.)* What the hell?

ENCINIA Now stand up.

BLAND *(Crying.)* All of this for a traffic signal. I swear to God. All
of this for a traffic signal. *(To bystander recording on their mobile
phone.)* Thank you for recording! Thank you! For a traffic signal –
slam me into the ground and everything! Everything!
I hope y'all feel good.

ENCINIA This officer saw everything.

FEMALE OFFICER: I saw everything.

BLAND I'm so glad to put that – you just got on the scene so whatever.

FEMALE OFFICER: I was…

BLAND No you wasn't you were pulling up. / No you didn't.

FEMALE OFFICER: No ma'am.

BLAND You didn't see everything leading up to it…

FEMALE OFFICER: You know what, I'm not talking to you.

BLAND You don't have to! You don't have to…

(Pause.)

ENCINIA 25-47 county. Send me a first-available, for arrest.

A simple gesture of hanging by the performers could also be used to signify what happened after this scene took place. Alternatively, it might be helpful to include in programme notes or conclude the live performance with a simple statement, either spoken or through a projection, that: 'two days after the arrest, Sandra Bland was found hanging in her police cell'.

MY WHITE BEST FRIEND

by Rachel De-Lahay

NB This speech is to be held and read aloud by the named actor as though her diary, written by somebody else.

First up, a request from the writer... Can we just do a quick audience reshuffle? All the girls need to be at the front. All brown, black, queer, disable girls, centre. All white, able-bodied men, fall back. Not to segregate. With our little shuffle we're just saying, we know what's going on out there, but in here, this space is safe and you are more than valued and loved. Thank you.

So... I am going to read something. Apparently.

My White Best Friend. By Rachel De-lahay.

Right. This is Rachel 'doing' me. If that makes sense? Hopefully it will. Okay...

Hi! My name is Ruth Minkley. I'm best friends with Rachel De-lahay.

Best.

I'm also an actor hence... And I'm stood here representing myself. Literally. And also every other white friend of Rachel's.

Ever.

In Birmingham, where Rachel is from, her friends were mainly black and Asian, but she doesn't see them that much nowadays. They text and FaceTime, and she goes back, though not as often as she'd like, cause, you know...life. So she misses them. A lot.

But it's okay cause we... The collective of me and Rachel's other white friends... *We* met, nearly thirteen years ago.

Wow. Thirteen years.

We've lived together, got drunk together, experimented with drugs together, fallen in love with each other, seen each other fall in love with others. Helped mend heartbreak. Fought. My god have we fought. Laughed, cried, sang, to Britney and Rihanna, at the top of our voices, in our bedrooms, in pyjamas, on an exclusive diet of Blossom Hill...

Rachel once held back my hair, as I threw up, on the night bus.

I was vomiting between my legs after having one too many free glasses of crystal in the VIP section of China Whites. I said it then, I'll say it again, Crystal is literally wasted on twenty-one-year-olds who drink lambrini when getting ready.

We started a diet together, once, eating an excellent three-bean casserole that I prepared. Then on our way to a gig Rachel nearly passed out on the tube from "weakness" and I had to get her off, and buy her a King-sized Twix.

I borrowed her dress on holiday and it looked better on me and she hated me for it.

Then the day Rachel found out she was going to be paid to rewrite her first ever play, I was with her. In Chanel on Bond Street.

We were staring at the life we wanted and when she got off the phone we sat down in front of a quilted, navy, lambskin, 2.55 flap bag and thought…*one step closer.*

Then a sales assistant started talking to us and somehow got us confused with people who were legitimately capable of buying said bag so we quickly left, and went to the Botanist where I bought us a Bellini. Mine orange, Rachel's red.

What I'm saying is, I can't replace her decades-long friendships from back home. I can't be Neetu or Daina, who are both fucking ace. I've met them, lots. But we have known each other for a really long time now and we are…family.

—

The first time I met her other 'family', her 'Daina and Neetu', they came down together for a birthday party of one of the girls from our Drama School. Well, they came down to see Rachel, and Rachel dictated the circumstances. So…we were gonna all hang for the first time.

I was a little nervous, as anyone is when they're about to meet the friends of your new *best* friend. You wonder if…it's gonna work, basically. If there'll be jealousy, a jostling of position. But there wasn't. Really. It was easy.

Me and Neetu got told off, quite vehemently, by Rachel for pouring and drinking Malibu and Coke in the back of Rachel's car, after we *promised* we wouldn't, cause… *'We understood there was literally no way to guarantee we wouldn't spill any."* Which we did. Lots.

But Neetu laughed which allowed me to laugh, as Neetu had known Rachel for way longer so… That was the start of cementing me and Neets.

Then Daina asked me where I was from, and I said Nottingham, and for the rest of the night I became Daphne – as in Frasier. And… I'm not gonna lie, I'm kinda easy. Nickname me, I'm yours. So yeah… that cemented us.

I was one of the girls.

Did I notice they were brown and black girls? Yes. Did I care? No.

—

MY WHITE BEST FRIEND

So we go to the party and, no judgement, Neetu and Daina peaked and crashed hard. I was in charge of pouring in the back of the car so I take a bit of responsibility but... I was still standing so...

Rachel had to put them both to bed and then came back down and it was back to being us, the drama school lot. And everyone rushed to tell Rachel how ace her Birmingham friends were, but, equally we were kinda okay with them being in bed and there being no more outsiders.

I think I said this to Rachel, as a way of flattering her. Exaggerating a kind of jealousy. And she smiled and pretended to be flattered.

And then we danced.

—

The next time they were down, they'd bought tickets to some club night in Elephant, that they'd had to book months in advance, with named DJs and Celebrity PAs and Singers or... I mean, I don't know. I'd never even heard of it. But I wasn't going anyway, cause I was hideously hung over and more than happy to spend the entire evening in pyjamas with zero plans.

Until Neetu and Daina arrived...

Then there was music and getting ready and Lambrinni, obvs. And then...yeah, I wanted to go.

So I asked. And of course everyone screamed YES. It was Daphne!

Even though sourcing an extra ticket proved nigh on impossible, but Daina knew someone, who knew someone so...

We're off. To a typical club, that was to be playing typical music... Only the whole thing was less than typical.

There was this queue outside that seemed to snake all the way around the building. And these cars, parked up front, blaring...bass. And these loud girls...in these...tiny... I mean, I'm all for short, shorts but... I dunno.

It just wasn't...typical.

No one was really drinking... Instead there were these moody guys stood in corners, blocking pathways and toilets to just stare and smoke.

Inside! Smoking?!

Beneath their hoodies and attitudes... And the girls weren't much different.

I didn't get the big deal. Why would you plan for this?

A song that me and Rachel had said was our song suddenly boomed out and Rach grabbed my hips and pushed me onto the dance floor but everyone was dancing so...wild, and I couldn't dance like...that, so I just...

I really was tired. And hung over and I reckoned it was just my time to crash.

But Neetu grabs my arm to try and make me dance with her... And Daina is like *Daphne! You need another shot!* But I didn't. I needed to go. And then Rachel saw it too. So she dropped me home.

In the car we mainly drove in silence. I thanked her. A lot. And apologized for being a *hassle*. And when we got home I said goodbye, as she was going back out, and then said *I love you, cause...*

And though she didn't say it back, she smiled, so...

—

Most recently, when Neetu and Daina came down, we had an impromptu house party. As in, we'd gone to the pub but then wanted to keep drinking for a long time after the pub closed.

So everyone ended up back at ours.

We're in the flat drinking, smoking, some people smoking things they shouldn't be. I'd guess I knew 85% of the people there. I think Rachel knew the same. But we had enough guy mates with us to feel safe about the fact that a few randoms' came back, so...

Music's playing, through my iPhone, then some smart alec thought to link up the sound to the TV for more volume. So my phone is switched off, the telly's switched on and it's late and on some 24hour news thing showing some sort of protest, which completely kills the vibe.

Rachel knew it was a Black Lives Matter protest against the murder of Alton Sterling; a man who was restrained by two officers and then filmed from several different angles, by several different members of the public, all showing the officers pinning down his arms and chest and head, and still then shooting him twice, dead.

She knew cause that was the reason Daina and Neetu had come down that day. The three of them had gone to the march.

I wasn't invited.

Had I been, I would have loved to go. But no one told me about it so I didn't know.

MY WHITE BEST FRIEND

Anyway, we're having this party and suddenly the news is on as opposed to Beyoncé and someone screams... *Where's the fucking music?* Then someone else goes... *What the fuck is this?!* And a third is like... *Why are they allowed to say that? Black lives matter? Like, Is that not racist? Like, why do they matter more?*

And I shrugged. Cause, again, I didn't know.

And Neetu and Daina looked really uncomfortable. And the silence that followed, that went on for what felt like a lifetime, was eventually filled with agreements, and *yeahs. It's a little aggressive, kinda exclusive...* Someone muttered how *we don't get a white history month...*which is true. Then Rachel got shouted across the room... *Are you kidding?!* And we're back to silence.

And awkward giggles and stifled laughs. And girls in their phones, pretending to text, like there's anyone to text at 1am. And if there is, why are you here? And in the background, on the news, name after name after name of other black men and women who'd been killed this year alone...

I had to switch it off.

I decided everyone was too drunk and high to deal with this conversation, so I turned the telly off and the music back on.

Rachel didn't have to thank me for that. She's my best friend.

—

She then sat in the corner of the room with Neetu and Daina, chastising herself for not having the words to explain to that idiot the point of Black Lives Matter. And as I joined them, I heard Neetu say... *Maybe not everyday us educating and not everyday them 'not knowing'. Maybe some days remembering Google is free.*

And Rachel nodded, and, wanting to support, I reminded them... *sometimes white people don't feel it's their place to speak about race. You know?*

And Neetu and Daina smiled.

They really are the best.

Then Neetu dragged Rachel to her feet to dance cause... Well, we really were all too drunk to talk about this.

—

I ended up in the garden that night for ages talking to one of the randoms, who was kinda funny and smart and looked a little like

177

Macaulay Culkin in a Terry Richardson photo shoot, which was, sadly, exactly my type back then. And by the time I came back in, the party was over. Everyone had left or gone to bed.

Then Rachel walks back in, in Pyjamas, to clear up the last of the rubbish, so me and 'McCauley' help. Then, when, Rachel bends over in front of him, he makes just an awkward joke about us being the last two girls, so him having pick of the bunch or something...

I don't even try and hear the ending; I've already got him his coat.

But he's now mortified, and apologises straight away, first to me and then to Rachel. Then, laughing nervously, he declares he was *obviously* kidding cause he liked me! And Rachel wasn't even really his type. Like he'd never even dated a black girl before. Not that he had a problem with black girls, it was just a fancying thing. Like, he wasn't really ever into girls with dark nipples. They just weren't his...thing.

Still holding his coat, Rachel now opened the door. He left. Then I went to bed. Then...

Remember when I said we fought?

Rachel called after me, asking if she could expect my support, ever?

I thought this was really unfair, as her two examples of me being unsupportive were when dealing with men who were just too stupid or awkward or drunk to even engage with, and they didn't deserve a response. You know?

I then looked up and Neetu and Daina were now in the doorway, in their pyjamas, Daina in a Black Lives Matter tee that Rachel looked at and then scoffed, mumbling something about *that not being the only time you weren't there.*

And I couldn't just stop so I continued, with...

I would have come on the march. If you wanted my support. I would have been there, but you never asked. You never told me. I didn't even know it was happening so how could I have? I'm not psychic.

And then she scoffed again.

Then Neetu passed me to get her and Daina some water and the room was now painfully quiet, so I carried on...

And I would have spoke up to that guy. About the black lives matter thing. But you already did. And it got awkward. And I'm not an academic. I don't know how to phrase things. I don't know the history to things, so I don't what to say.

MY WHITE BEST FRIEND

And the nipple thing? That's just blatant, ignorant racism. So what could I say to that?!

And then...

I just felt horrible. And kept thinking, why is my friend making me feel like this? And her friends were just watching and clearly thinking things. And I was like, this is stupid. I'm not the enemy. I'm not racist. I've done nothing wrong. And yet I was here being shouted at like I have. And I thought I'd never do this to her. I'd never make anyone feel like this.

Ever.

Then Rachel said...

Sorry.

Cause I was right. It wasn't my problem. She said...

Sorry for allowing a boy's stupid comments to get to me. I know I'm better than that. I'm tougher than that. So, sorry. Sorry for allowing myself to get drunk and become weak and vulnerable to those comments. Sorry for forgetting there's no time for that. There's only time for remembering to look after yourself, cause no one else will. Sorry for wondering if he called me fat, if you would have been more vocal, cause that's beside the point.

And sorry for hoping the murder of young lives, constantly, consistently, would outrage you like it did me and make you want to investigate and shout and scream and be at centre of every protest ever. Like I had to be.

Sorry for not always getting that you and your friends sometimes want me to yourself, because you love me and love spending time with me, and when that means me being the only minority in a room, again...? Shake it off!

Sorry for daring to take you to a party where you were the minority.

Sorry for not for seeing that you wouldn't like that, be comfortable with that, at all and for not trying harder, to come up with a better, safer lie in advance as to why you shouldn't join us in Elephant. Sorry for being disappointed with your not getting the "big deal" and not being capable of saying to you, when I dropped you home, I love you. Cause I do. I really do. I just get angry and need to learn to monitor that better. Cause none of this is your problem. None of it. So sorry for assuming you'd give a fuck, when you're the embodiment of every privilege I smack up against every day. With your face that's celebrated in every corner of this earth...

You seek out "normal" shampoo and don't think to question it whilst I sit here like...man, that must be ace being normal.

That's Rachel's apology.

Except it wasn't cause...

That fight didn't happen. At all. I just went to bed. And Rachel let me. Cause this is the fight you and your white best friend will never have. Cause how do you say to someone you love... You let me down.

How do you ask your white best friend to try and visibly give a damn? Change your profile picture, share that post, march! Knowing it will make them feel uncomfortable? How could you ever put your white best friend on stage and remind them that they're part of the problem? If you love them? If you never want anyone to feel for even a moment how you feel living in this world everyday.

So we don't discuss it. Which means I never got to say...

I'm sorry.

I'm sorry when you spoke your mind, I shuffled and shifted uncomfortable with the dialogue. I'm sorry that on gutsier days I argued points defending myself first and foremost, as a woman, a white woman, struggling to see the difference. I'm sorry I never thought to educate myself privately, and fight, not even along side you, but in front of you, cause maybe you're tired.

This is the most uncomfortable I've ever been on stage. And I don't like it. One bit.

But maybe that's okay. Maybe not everyday enjoying our privileges and coasting through life, comfortable. Maybe some days putting ourselves out there for somebody else. Standing up, loudly, visibly for some one less privileged and baring the brunt of the brazen misogyny, racism and homophobia that can incur.

I am not that white woman. Yet. These words aren't my words. They are a request, an offering, from my best friend who thinks if we have the ability to reshuffle and change a small space like The Bush theatre, so quickly, into a safe space, we have the ability to change to the world.

And, having had a bit of time off up until now, asking me to do my bit.

Thank you for this experience,

FATHER'S DAY

by Max Kolaru

Act One

A dishevelled plot in Kensal Green Cemetery. **PHILIP** *arrives to tend his Father's grave, armed with shovel, shears, and fork, as the grave has not been tended in nearly a year. He feels a space in his jacket, before looking down at the overgrown ground, shovel in hand. There's a distant rumble of thunder.*

URMA, *his sister, arrives, with large umbrella to shield her from the heat on this unusually hot day in Summer.*

PHILIP Did you see that?

(They look out into the distance.)

URMA What?

PHILIP I saw someone moving, over there. *(Pointing.)*

URMA Will be someone putting down flowers.

PHILIP Did you see?

URMA No.

PHILIP These places give me the creeps. Bones, dust an wondering souls.

URMA The dead don't wonder.

PHILIP I'm talking about the soul, not the body. They say if you weight a person, just before they pass, an just after, they weight 21 grams less. That's the weight of the soul that's departed the body. I used to know someone who was trying to communicate with the other side. Said he was on the verge of breaking through, contacting the dead. He said he'd almost crossed over.

URMA What did he see?

PHILIP Dun know? He got the sack for having sex with a woman on his office desk, an we lost touch. *(Beat.)* I seen it again! Maybe we should come back tomorrow. *(Turning.)*

URMA They're laying the gravestone for the anniversary tomorrow. The plot needs to be cleared, today – there's people coming, to pay their respects – To Remember.

PHILIP *(Turning back. Moves some of the weeds with the shovel.)* It looks different.

URMA You sure it's the right one?

PHILIP I asked at the gate, got the plot reference.

URMA

PHILIP *(Looking around.)* Who took the cross? His cross had his name, the date, everything.

URMA It would've rotted away by now/

PHILIP Not in a year – It hasn't even bin a year yet. It'll be a year tomorrow, wood don't rot down in under a year, metal don't rot down at all. Metal'll only get rusty.

URMA Maybe one of the cemetery staff – a grave digger.

PHILIP Grave diggers dig graves, they don't rob crosses. Unless – one a them took it – outta spite/

URMA One a them?

PHILIP Whoever did it to Dad

URMA Followed us into the cemetery, when we were *(Beat.)* burying Dad, an come back to steal a cross/

PHILIP You hear bout it all the time, them people who mark-up Jewish graves, put pork round them, or spray swastikas/

URMA Dad wasn't Jewish/

PHILIP I'm jus' saying – it could happen –

URMA Do you wanna go back to the gate?

PHILIP We shouldna left it so long. It's all ivy, an brambles strangling everything. *(Tries to pull some up, but gets stung.)* Bloody stinging nettles an weeds, you can't see weeds for nuffin' else.

URMA He was always partial to a bit a weed –

PHILIP I'm going back to the gate – Will you be ok – by yourself?

URMA If the dead could hurt you, they wouldn't be dead would they!

PHILIP If anyone has stolen the cross, an try come back, I'll be waiting for them. *(Shovel up.)* If I woulda been there, five minutes earlier – Dad – didn't stan' a chance – by himself/

URMA

PHILIP *(Beat.)* Back in a mo then. *(Rests the shovel against an overgrown bush, before leaving for the front gate.)*

(The glaring heat becomes overcast, with a refreshing breeze starting to blow. The sun soon returns with a vengeance, casting a spotlight on the plot before widening out into brilliant sunshine.)

*(**URMA** opens her wide umbrella to shield away some of the soaring heat.)*

*(A sound of movement and shuffling in the undergrowth is heard. **URMA** slowly lowers her large umbrella, in defensive mode.)*

PHILIP *(Jumps from behind.)* Boo! *(It backfires as **URMA** nearly jooks him in the eyeball.)*

URMA *Idiot!*

PHILIP Girl – You nearly strike me eye!

URMA Idiot – /

PHILIP I seen you all with the umbrella, like Zulu Dawn – Thought you said the dead can't hurt you –

URMA I heard something – A living something/

PHILIP I told you – I said we should come back tomorrow, when there's family aroun'. I ain't one a them white people in those horror movies – I ain't sticking round to get mash up!

URMA So pick up the damn shovel and let's start. *(Beat.)* Is it Dad's?

PHILIP Definitely. She looked at me funny. Like she thought I was claiming she was lying. Or like – *"If you came more often, you'd know".*

URMA She probably gets asked the same question a million times – From people, who don't come, regularly.

PHILIP We're not jus' people – Sis. We're Family. An I never come 'ere to be judged.

URMA You're paranoid. An I said I was never coming back here at all. Not until.

PHILIP It's nearly bin a year, you need ta dun dat now – Sis.

URMA It ain't even started – No witnesses. No suspects. No arrests. No investigation. No fingerprints – No nuffin.

PHILIP There *was* an investigation – Sis. Searches, forensics, statements, descriptions/

URMA That resulted in what?

PHILIP There weren't nothing concrete – Sis. Nothing that could stick/

URMA

PHILIP

URMA *(Beat.)* Where we supposed to start?

PHILIP *(Beat.)* Should we say – a prayer or something, first?

URMA We're not religious/

PHILIP He was. A Good Christian.

URMA When it suited him. Made sure he was at church come Harvest Festival, without fail, when they were serving food. The best Hindu, down at the Neasden temple when they were celebrating Sewa Day. First at the Synagogue on Holocaust Memorial Day when they were serving tea /

URMA Down at the Mosque when they were feeding the community.

PHILIP What can I say. He was a man of the World, there's no denying that/

(The sound of a distant steel band from Ladbroke Grove drifts through the air.)

URMA He should be here now, getting ready for Carnival. Putting on his little suit an ting, the kerchief an the watch chain, looking nice and decent. Like when they all did firs' land in this wicked Country. Never a day out of a suit – to be laying face down in his own/

PHILIP Not here Sis –

URMA An nobody aint' seen a thing. In broad daylight. One o clock in the big afternoon, on a public street, on a weekday an nobody ain't seen a thing/

PHILIP Not Now – Sis. *(Beat.)* Let's sing something then: *'When the Saints Come Marching In'*. Or: *'Morning Has Broken'*. I know them ones. Dad liked them. *(Starts singing before she can protest.)*

"Morning Has Broken,
Like the First Summer,
Blackbirds are Singing,
Like the First Dawn,
Praise Every Morning,
Praise for Creation,
Praise for the… Something Else,
Of a New Day".

*(**URMA** is just looking on him. He nudges her to join in.)*

This one's more upbeat, Sis. Come on, join in – For Dad.

*"Oh When the Saints
Come Marching In,
Oh When the Saints Come Marching In"*

(He nudges her again.)

URMA *(Reluctant, and said rather than sung.)* I-Want-To-Be-Among-That-Number.

PHILIP *(Finishing with upbeat enthusiasm.)*

"Oh When Those Saints Come Marching Home".

(Lifts the shovel, marching with it, first on the spot, then around the plot, until his marching comes to an abrupt halt.)

URMA You quite finished.

PHILIP You gotta try an lighten the mood – Sis. It ain't good for your heart, to be stressing 24-7 /

URMA What should we do, forget we had a Dad, forget what he looked like, the las' time we saw him.

PHILIP We're doing the bes' thing to remember him. This – Getting all this cleared/

URMA An anniversary, with corn beef an cucumber sandwiches, Saturday Soup in thermal cups, hot sauce an fishcakes, curry chicken an a bowl a souse, ain't gonna bring him back/

PHILIP It'll give people something to refocus on/

URMA I don't want people to refocus. I wan' it to be fresh in their minds.

PHILIP There was a march – Nobody's saying it ain't in people's heads no more. But going roun' an roun'– You gotta come up for air – Or – It chokes you dead – Sis. *(Tries to dig down into the soil heavily, but the ground is too dry.)* Then they've really won. *(Beat.)* I'm gonna find some water, to try soften the ground. *(He walks away with the shovel.)*

(The wind begins to kick up. The sun that has been a brilliant glow becomes sharp and severe. The sound of distant thunder rumbles.)

URMA Philip! Philip! *(Shout.)* Philip!

Act Two

The scene is as before, but more overcast, forming shades and shadows across the cemetery. **URMA** *looks distressed. When* **PHILIP** *returns it startles her greatly.*

PHILIP So you do care/

URMA You stupid Bastard! Course I bloody care, what you trying a do, jus' wondering off!

PHILIP Since Dad – passed – You're just always, on one.
They done everything they could/

URMA So one year on, why's it still the same.

PHILIP You can't, you can't carry them things round with you –

URMA What happened when you went to the police station

PHILIP Don't question me like that – Sis/

URMA What happened/

PHILIP I can't remember – Sis, it was a long time ago – I ain't dwelling on/

URMA Weren't they all looking to arrest *you*. Didn't they all, take your finger prints, an photograph you, an was looking for DNA on your shoes/

PHILIP DNA – Sis. What I tell you bout DNA. It stands for, Don't-Know-Anything, so they make it up. They knew they had nothing on me, that was all wasting time – Time wasting – Sis/

URMA You went in there for help, you went in there bleeding, with blood on you, needing help, screaming for help/

PHILIP I'm not keen to bring it up – Sis/

URMA An not just blood. Not just any old blood. Our Father's Blood. *(Beat, voice cracking.)* What did you have in your hands – What did you have!

(The rumble of thunder grows louder, threatening to drown her out.)

PHILIP It ain't getting us nowhere, remembering all dat – Bringing it all up, again. This is about, moving forward/

URMA There ain't no future without no pass yah narh/

PHILIP Sis – Please/

URMA His Heart – My Father – Your Father – Our Father's own heart!

PHILIP It wasn't his heart Sis/

URMA Lung then/

PHILIP Sis! Please!

URMA A kidney. A Liver. A Spleen. What you had in your hand – Was part of him – Part of a human being – An you went to the police for help, cos they cut him down, outside the police station. An when you went in – bleeding, with a p-part of our Father, what did they say. What did they say – *What!*

PHILIP You're getting hysterical now Sis. *(Beat.)* I can't remember what they said/

URMA Black on Black Crime – *"Who have you stabbed then"?* That's exactly what they said. An you was screaming for them to come outside. Screaming for them to stem the blood, stem the flow, the flood – to use something to stop up the hole, a hole so big that you could put your han' in it. An they said you was being aggressive, pinned you down, handcuffed *you*. Stepped on my Father's Heart, slid in it, an accused you of pushing them, attacking a police officer, was looking to charge *you*. An My Father was out there, on the street, he was out there on the street. Outside the police station, on the street – an he was dying – An you can't remember that – *You carn remember dat!*

(He begins to use the shears, cutting through the ivy roughly.)

PHILIP They did all they could. *(Beat.)* When they finally believed me... But –

URMA But what –

PHILIP But. It was. It was/

URMA It was too late –

PHILIP You know it was – Sis. I tried, I tried to do all I could –

URMA But you didn't do enough! Now did you

PHILIP *(Shears in her direction.)* I did what I could. We marched didn't we. We marched all the way through Paddington – Paddington to Westminster. Staged a protest outside the police station. Refused to move – Refused to move, until we got justice/

URMA Only – We didn't get any – Did We – Marching don't do shit but wear down your shoes/

PHILIP An what would you have done – Bun down the police station, kill every las' white man an women in sight –

URMA It ain about every white man an woman in sight – The people who did it was on the CCTV. The CCTV attached to the side of the damn police station. The same CCTV that the police claim held footage that accidentally got destroyed, but showed nothing anyway. An a CCTV in the duty area, that weren't recording, cause – It was due for maintenance. But it did manage to record you, acting aggressively towards two police officers an apparently attempting to assault them/

PHILIP – They know dat was rubbish – That was all dropped – It don't help to dwell on it/

URMA Is that you talking – Or your white wife/

PHILIP Daz out of order – Sis. Don't bring her into it. Sophie's bin with us all the way. A rock. Wasn't it her that found the solicitor. Made all the phone calls when we woz falling apart. Liaised with the victim support/

URMA To get us the little few thousand pounds/

PHILIP It was something – Sis. It paid for all this, the funeral, the hall an the food after. An still some left over for the gravestone for *this* anniversary.

URMA This ain't 12 Years A Slave yah narh – She ain't Brad Pitt come to save all us poor ignorant negros!

(A loud strike of thunder follows a brief flash of lightning and a sharp gust that blows across the cemetery.)

PHILIP She was there Urma – While you was spouting out revolution to the world an whoever would listen, she was handling practical business – At home/

URMA Chat with your brain Philip – Not wid your cock!

PHILIP You too mean an vicious. That's why you ain't got no man, Black, White, Orange or Green in the last eight years/

URMA Before any – None!

PHILIP Waz dat suppose ta mean.

URMA Go ask your wife – seeing as she's so clever.

PHILIP *(Beat.)* You know what – Sis. *(Beat.)* There's a lot of work to do. Lezs just get on with it. Don't let one random act sully all your life. It's only that that gives them the upper han'.

URMA Random! You really don't get it – do you?

PHILIP Listen, I get that you're angry – I was angry too, but you're letting it become *you*. When las' did you have a laugh.

URMA I'll laugh when we get justice –

PHILIP There ain't no justice – Sis. Didn't you get the 80's memo – There's Just Us. So you can keep moping roun' waiting for justice an for all the white people to get what's coming to them, come Judgement Day, when we *"All Gone be Free"*, but hear what – Sis. It ain't coming. These people are powerful people. Bin powerful for centuries. Powerful people don't give up their power for nuffin. You see dat mobile phone you got, always on it, agitating, contacting this legal person, to try an find this an that legal loophole so you can try reopen the case. The same people – The same race a white people you're trying a fight against, is privately listening to every word you say. Look at what they did to the Lawrences. A Good upright God Fearing Family that they were trying a find dirt on, all the while pretending they was doing everything to further the course of justice. But really an truly, doing everyting they could to mek sure the racists that did murder Stephen Lawrence got away scot free.

URMA But the Family kept pushing, pushing to get justice, no matter what/

PHILIP You ain't Lady Doreen. You ain't got the stamina, you ain't stuck to nothing in your whole life – part from this. *Your* fight for Dad – Your cause/

URMA *Our Fight! Our Family's fight/*

PHILIP Dropped out a accountancy after eight months, dropped outta banking after six. Could only make it two months in insurance sales and ran out on *Our* so called family when you was up in Ghana, trying a find out who you were. Some afrocentric rubbishness – That's why you're hanging onto this –Sis, this, cause – it's the only thing you've managed to stick at for over twelve months. *(Beat.)* Not even 12 months. It'll be 12 months tomorrow. An you can't make up for feeling guilty by holding onto something that – that's gone Sis/

URMA That's *your* guilt talking/

PHILIP *(Downs his tools.)* Guilt! What I gotta feel guilty for/

URMA You know full well/

PHILIP I ain't guilty – Sis. What the hell I got to be guilty for. I'm jus' trying to get it into your *(Breathes.)* head that they don't

191

care bout us. You think they care that one unimportant Black Father – Our Father get kill by a bunch a racist dogs. It could be every las' Black Father for all they care. Everytime one of us get cut down, they're clapping their hands; One less nigger to have to deal wid.

URMA Too shame to admit/

PHILIP Shame bout what – Sis!

URMA That you could go, marry into dat/

PHILIP Why you got to always bring it down to dat level.

URMA They can't kill us off – so they're diluting us off the face of the planet – Getting us to produce more fuzzy headed, light brown, acceptable children./

(A crash of thunder.)

PHILIP *(A Beat before he starts 'gardening' again.)* There's a white person in all of us – Sis. Even ones as Black as you. Where you tink you get dat sharp nose from! *(Beat.)* You know how Dad love a white woman. Even if it was only for four months at a time, then he'd come back to Mum's potatoes an dumplings. Dublin, Germany, Wales, you know Dad spent nuff time in those places. An you know he never did sleep alone neither. *(Beat.)* Hating all a them won't bring him back – Sis. It'll jus' eat away at your soul.

URMA They're soulless/

PHILIP The people that did that to Dad – /

URMA They're not people, not human, they can't be. Jus' cause they're walking on two legs, talk in human language, an take on human form, don't make them human/

PHILIP So what are they then, 3/5th of a human, like what they said about us in them old slave times/

URMA – Them old slaves times! Shot our pregnant women, skinned them alive, split them open, raped them young, buried their babies head high in the ground just to see how far they could kick them off; strapped us to carts an mek us pull them like ox. Mek us carry dog shit in our mouths; burned us alive, pushed explosives up us, just to watch us explode – An daz all you can say – dem ole slave times/

PHILIP Give it up – Sis. There's good an bad in everyone, it's as plain an simple as dat – There's only two kin's a people in this worl'. The one's that would let you on the bus, when you got insufficient change, an the one's that would drive on an let you stan' up in the pouring rain – So please don't talk about my wife Sophie,

particularly as she can cook Saturday Soup, which you can't.
She also does mek a mean peas an rice.

URMA *(Beat.)* Iz rice an peas, an your Sophie's so call peas an rice, aint got na tast'/

PHILIP Her chicken's passable/

URMA That ain't got no tast' neither.

PHILIP Nobody likes it spicey anymore – Sis. Black people have gone off pepper, you ask anyone/

URMA She probably don't even wash da chicken, fore she cooks it/

PHILIP They said not to do that anymore, it spreads bacteria/

URMA What you tink bleach is for!

PHILIP I'm speaking plain – Sis. An I might have a white wife to come home to, but you're jus' probably gonna be a barren old spinster. Who me an my white wife are gonna have to take in, when all your cats turn on you.

URMA *(Beat.)* Dad said cats are the only thing that keep the mice down.

PHILIP *(Beat.)* Dad ain't around no more. *(Beat.)* Sis, I don't wanna fight with you. We done enough fighting this past year. *(Beat.)* *(Looking up at the sheet lighting.)* We're not making progress, an it looks like it's gonna *"rain on our heads"*.

URMA The las' thing Dad said to me…

PHILIP Keep it to yourself – Sis. It won't change anything/

URMA The las' thing he said was…

(There's a loud clap of thunder. The heaven's open. **URMA** *and* **PHILIP** *try their best to shield under the large umbrella.)*

Act Three

The sudden onslaught of rain is beginning to quell. **PHILIP** *looks gingerly out from under the cover of the umbrella.*

PHILIP I wan'ed more. I didn't wanna be stuck in Dad's beat up ole house on the corner of Edgware Road forever. Sophie's people, have got a bit put away.

URMA It's a beat up ole house, but its Dad's beat up ole house. An for the most part, it was full a love.

PHILIP *(Picking up the shovel.)* An all you need is love, isn't it Sis. Like I love Sophie, an all of our light brown acceptable children.

URMA *(Beat.)* I love my nieces an nephews, even when they are acting stink.

PHILIP I know you do Sis.

URMA *(Puts down the umbrella, picks up the shears.)*

PHILIP Member back in da day – Sis – Jus' went pictures innit. From Flash Gordon was up there on that screen an you had your little curly whirly or toffee bar in your han', nothing seemed it could touch you. Running back to Dad, to yam the Saturday Soup, always way beta than Mum's.

URMA Southbank, when Dad used to take us up there to see the skateboarders. I went up there last week. They had on this Festival of London. There was a plastic bag from Dub Vendor behind a glass. An these photographs; boys body popping in the street in Adidas an high tops. Crowds dancing to Soul 2 Soul at the Africa Centre; a group a Black girls dancing on the corner a Latimar Road, in kabechis, an pleated skirts, 1976 Carnival /

PHILIP You know the young people sporting Kangols now, calling them 'bucket hats'! Cheek – It's all new for old Sis/

URMA Dad had a stall at Carnival, you member, 1986; How proud we was, helping him serve up the food. That's *Our Youth, Our Hope* – All behind glass, like dead museum pieces. An they're still cutting us down in the street, like we don't matter, like we never mattered/

PHILIP *(Standing close to her, arm comforting round her shoulder.)* It's a circle Sis – All the crap that's getting done to us, is gone come all the way back round.

URMA I didn't wanna cry, I didn't come here to cry. *I-don't-want-to-cry.*

PHILIP You cry it out Sis. You let it out. Everytime I turn on the TV there's a white person crying. Every single night, them a ball! You never see Black people cry. We're unimportant – In the Metro, I see some big spread about two white men, supposed to be pioneers of dancehall!– bringing it to London, in big 2015– you could believe dat! We're invisible.

URMA So invisible, we can't even register on a CCTV camera, outside a police station. *He was attacked, outside a police station! How could that happen. How could that be. (Fights back more tears.)*

PHILIP *(Beat.)* That's what I said – at the time.

URMA What?

PHILIP *(Beat.)* Dad, ended up, outside the police station, but/

URMA *(Gaining composure.)* Butts are for arseholes Philip – What you talking about?

PHILIP *(Beat.)* We were out with *My Dad, My Father* – An they were talking the piss –

URMA Who?

PHILIP *(Beat.)* Sometimes the universe smiles on you, Sis. An sometimes it shits in your face. An you can only take, so much. Dad was outside the police station, that's where he ended up.

URMA *(Puts down the shears.)* From where?

PHILIP

URMA *From where Philip?*

PHILIP Listen. I ain't no monkey, I ain't no coon, an I ain't no nigger. An if I'm going back to Africa, I'm going back on my own terms, not coz some white racists say I should.

URMA

PHILIP *(Beat.)* You know me. I like a woman with perfect feet. Mos' Black women have got, real ugly feet; toes like pieces a ginger, stuck on the end of some tree bark – not Sophie.

URMA An mos' white women blow up like balloons come 35, an look a hundred at 38- What you trying a say – Philip.

PHILIP *(Starting to dig with a passion.)* I'm clearing this space, people can at least stan' aroun' here. Pay their respects, remember

Dad how he was – That's all he woulda wanted. Everything looking decent. Dad was always decent. Always in a suit, like when he firs' did come over. A yout' looking smart. Not like the yout' of today. Jeans halfway down dem backside – Shuffling like they jus' did come outta jail, wid something to hide –

URMA What you saying – Philip?

PHILIP I was with Dad. Me an Dad. But Sophie, was with us.

URMA –

PHILIP We were coming round by Bermondsey side, coz Dad wan'ed to take a trip up to St Katherine's Docks. He always had to be travelling, could never stay one place. But. There was an idiot, mouthing off, right in the middle a the street. Black dis, you Black dat, *"Get your dirty hands off our white women"*. Then he come up to Dad, pointing his han' in Dad's face. Messing with his watch chain. Dad wan'ed ta let it go, said the boy was "Ignorant". I got in front a Dad. An Dad was pleading "Let it go Son". An I woulda. For Dad's sake, for Sophie's sake – Then five a them come up, with bottles – An dragged Dad from behind me. *(Beat.)*

URMA What you mean – Dragged Dad from behind you?

PHILIP Just that. It was jus' an ordinary day out Urma. One a them was even carrying a plastic bag, from Morrisons/

URMA What you talking about They dragged Dad from behind you an all you saw was a plastic bag from Morrisons/

PHILIP You don't understan'. They were all round me. Two a them was holding me. One a them put the bag over my head, I couldn't breath – An Sophie was screaming – I could hear her screaming – An I couldn't breath/

URMA *What about Dad!*

PHILIP I could hear him, struggling, an fighting – An I could hear them smashing the bottles/

URMA What was Sophie doing/

PHILIP Sophie – she was helpless/

URMA She woulda seen – She woulda seen something, anything – What did she see/

PHILIP It was all a panic – It was done so fast/

URMA Fast enough for one a them to cuss you from the other side of the street. Fast enough for one a them to come up to you. Fas'

enuff for five a then to surround you. Put a bag over your head –
That ain't fast – That's time – That's time enough to do something
– Do something – Anything. Fast enough to See what's going on –
Who's doing it/

PHILIP I woulda taken everyone a them slashes, everyone a them.
He was in shreds… Shreds Sis. Sophie was screaming at them –
Screaming at them to stop/

URMA *She was speaking to them!*

PHILIP I carried him to that police station. I never had no breath,
but I carried him, my knees buckled outside, coz he was all over me,
all down me –

URMA You said it was just you an Dad – Sophie woulda seen
something – She would/

PHILIP I shoulda listened to Dad Sis – I shoulda let it go –
I shoulda let it go… But they were saying racist…the thing's they
were saying… About Dad. About Sophie, the Mother of my children
– Sophie's the mother of my children, she blames herself. For being
there, for causing it. What would people say… Sis – that was *Our
Father*… An I was defending him, an her…

URMA We've been looking for evidence, searching, hoping, praying
– All this Time – An all along – She spoke to them –
Had time to see them good –

PHILIP I'm not putting her through that anymore, she's done all
she could – She has nightmares/

URMA *Nightmares*!– What about Dad Philip – Dad – Justice for
Dad – For us.

PHILIP There ain't no justice for us. The police questioned me
an her, for hours on end – I've questioned her, time an time again.
So much that. *(Beat.)* I thought the relationship was gonna dun.
But I've stuck with her, we're stuck it out, an there's nothing more
we can do –

URMA You know the last thing Dad said to me/

PHILIP Sis/

URMA The last thing he said was "*We Are We*"/

PHILIP What/

URMA "*We Are We*", an we could do anything

PHILIP That's not the las' thing he said Sis. *(Beat.)* The las' thing he said, was when I was... I was holding his head – Trying to hold it up...trying to hold it together... And I didn't know what to say, to say... I knew he was... An I wan'ed to try an make him feel better... I... I asked him how he was feeling... An he said..."*I'm feeling fine, tank you*". An he looked down at his watch chain. An that was it. When I wen into that police station, I had the watch chain in my han', told them to search it for DNA. They asked me if I'd stolen it, said my prints would be all over it. I took it back to that station, three weeks after, for them to look for evidence, cause we had nothing but that – They took one look at it and said it was useless, inadmissible – said I was wasting my time, and there's.

URMA We lost the watch chain, haven't been able to find it/

PHILIP It's not lost. *(Beat.)* I slipped it into Dad's pocket, day of the funeral. When they opened the coffin. *(Beat.)* It didn't look like Dad anymore, it wasn't him. The only thing about him, that looked like him – was the watch chain, so I put it in.

URMA But Philip, it woulda had evidence on it. It would have.

PHILIP The police said it was useless.

URMA Philip, they also tried to claim that you assaulted them – But you didn't.

PHILIP I know that Sis.

URMA So – Dad's watch chain. It *would* have had evidence on it, vital evidence.

PHILIP I believed what they were saying. *(Beat.)* I'm the useless one.

URMA Philip. We can get the watch chain, back. We need to get it back.

PHILIP We're powerless Sis. There's nothing we can do.

URMA I ain't powerless. *(Gaining composure.)* I'm from a people that did raise nations and civilizations. Created the lightbulb, the traffic light, the space toilet, the ironing board, an the damn lemon squeezer! Gave the world astronomy an science and the first race to successfully sew up a person's heart! A people that could talk through telepathy, speak to each other for miles across expanses of water, through just whispers and drums. A people dat did fight, 450 years of Slavery an genocide. An we still fighting. Still Here. Still Alive!

PHILIP So what we suppose ta do/

URMA We need to – get Dad back – Exhume him – dig up/

PHILIP I know what exhume means, and no way – You can't do that Sis – You can't jus', raise up the – An the, the smell an/

URMA They'll be ways of doing it, Philip, ways that can make it alright/

PHILIP Bringing back, the dead Sis, can't never be alright.

URMA Not just, the dead Philip, Our Dad. *(Hugs him.)* An you were right, I said the dead can't hurt you – But I'm gonna mek damn sure it hurts them racists, who took way Our Father.

PHILIP It's not gonna be that simple Sis/

URMA Right here in Kensal Green cemetery, Marcus Garvey was buried; It's the last resting place for Mary Seacole. An right here, in Kensal Green, Kelso Cochrane – murdered by racist, an nobody charged – And despite all that racism, and slaughter, we still here. No wonder when white people see us they does always look so frightened. It must be like seeing a ghost/

(A deafening clap of thunder.)

PHILIP Why you got to be talking about ghosts in a place like this!!

URMA What you 'fraid for a bit a thunder an rain – Like you made a salt! Come the Revolution, Where you gonna be – Hiding behind your white wife's skirt –

(Another deafening clap of thunder.)

If the souls of our people can come back, let them come – Let them get the justice they never had – the justice they deserve – After the service tomorrow, an we've laid the gravestone, I'm ringing another solicitor. I'm not giving up. Come on. I gotta get home an make the corn beef sandwiches otherwise Mum's gonna kill me.

PHILIP *Wot about the plot – We can't leave it like this.*

URMA "*We Are We*" member – People can take us as they find us.

PHILIP *(Beat.)* You really think we can… You know. With Dad

URMA Yes. I'm positive. *(She leaves.* **PHILIP** *follows.)*

*(***PHILIP** *returns to the plot, armed with shovel. He feels a space in his jacket, and brings out a small bottle of white rum. He takes a long drink before spreading libations over the ground. A warm grumble of thunder ripples.* **PHILIP** *looks up to the sky.* **URMA** *returns; takes a long drink of the rum; spreading libations also.)*

(Thunder rumbles, under the music of a steel band.)

URMA *Come on.*

*(**PHILIP** follows after a short while.)*

PHILIP *(Calling to **URMA**.)* What about reparations – they owe us billions – there must be a legal ting you could start…

Curtain.

HIS LIFE MATTERS

by Yolanda Mercy

LIZ and CAT are in the reception room of their Doctors surgery.

LIZ   it seems that

CAT   ...

LIZ   that despite the fact

CAT   ...

LIZ   despite everything

CAT   ...

LIZ   that you want to

CAT   ...

LIZ   you think it would be a good idea to

CAT

LIZ   to

CAT   – not here

LIZ   – then where?

Beat.

CAT is about to say something, but then stops.

LIZ   where?

CAT stands up and is about to leave.

LIZ   typical

CAT walks towards to the door.

LIZ   when things get a little bit. Just that little

Beat.

CAT   shit

LIZ   what?

CAT   shit... When things get a bit shit

LIZ

CAT   when things get a bit shit, I leave

LIZ   – me!

Pause..

CAT stops turns around and looks at LIZ. LIZ looks out towards the audience.

Extended Pause.

CAT walks over to her. CAT is about to speak.

Tannoy: Could Mr Alufebi please go to room 3

Beat.

They both awkwardly smile while Mr Alufebi walks past.

Beat.

CAT searches in her pocket, and finds chalk in her pocket. She sits next to LIZ and offers it to her.

Beat.

CAT   Hungry?

Pause.

LIZ looks at the chalk in CAT's hands, looks disgusted – then smirks.

CAT   I thought you might be

LIZ   – I am.

CAT   I won't tell

Pause.

LIZ is tempted.

CAT   you know you want to

LIZ looks at the chalk.

Extended Pause.

LIZ looks away (to the left), but puts her right hand out for the chalk. CAT puts it in her hand.

Pause.

LIZ smiles, pulls the chalk towards her face opens her mouth and is about to eat it.

Pause.

She looks out towards the audience, then at her stomach.

Extended Silence.

She gives the chalk back to CAT.

Pause.

LIZ   you know I can't!

CAT   – I just thought that you…
that it would…that I could make you happy

LIZ

CAT   Sorry

Tannoy: Could Mrs De Silva please go to room 1

CAT   Liz… I'm sorry

LIZ

Extended Pause.

CAT   I'm sorry that I'm not supportive enough, that my mind can't extend to regular, clear apologies. That when things get tuff, get that little bit tuff I leave.*(Pause.)* I just…it's just…this isn't what I'd…what we'd expected. It's not what we expected

LIZ   I know

CAT   so you can understand that I'm

LIZ   angry?

CAT   upset…

Beat.

CAT   fuck it… I'm scared. I'm fucking scared

LIZ   we

CAT   what?

LIZ   We. *(Beat.)* I'm just as scared as you. We are scared.

Beat.

CAT   so why don't we just

LIZ   – No!

Pause.

LIZ   we aren't giving him away

Extended Silence.

LIZ puts her hands on her stomach.

LIZ   I've always dreamed about being a protector. Having
               something that needs me. *(Beat.)* Relies on me. Cats.
               Dogs. You *(she glances at her stomach)* him. Having a
               purpose, a reason to wake up everyday knowing that
               someone else relies on me. It makes me feel *(beat)*
               important.

Extended Pause.

LIZ   I understand that you want to leave. I do too. This place
               smells like piss and dead people.

CAT snorts.

LIZ   But before we do *(Beat.)* Before we leave. *(Beat.)* I need
               to know where we stand. Where I stand. *(Beat.)* Before
               we leave. *(Beat.)* Before you leave. Where. Do. I. Stand?

Pause.

Tannoy: Could Mr Thompson go to room 8

They sit in awkward silence.

LIZ starts to get her things together and prepares to leave.

CAT   This place really does smell like piss.

LIZ still starts to pack.

CAT   Maybe it's a metaphor for life...that no matter where
               you are someone will always piss on your parade

LIZ puts her coat on.

CAT   That great things...things that are meant to be exciting

LIZ does up her jacket.

CAT   like Nando's... Nando's being delivered by Deliveroo...
               (Beat.) or having a baby. *(Beat.)* ... Your first baby

LIZ puts her scarf on.

CAT   With your beautiful fucking girlfriend, can be pissed
and shat on by fear.

LIZ puts her hat on.

CAT   Liz, I'm fearful. Ok *(Beat.)* I'm really fucking fearful that
our son, our fucking disabled son to be. Will be stereotyped
cause of the way that he looks… The way that he is. That
every single time that he leaves the flat, the world will
see a label. Will project, a distorted painting on him…
of…of a…a black thug, a potential thief, drug dealer or
murder. That on the outside, he depicts everything that
the Daily Mail warns us about 'black youth'…but…but on
the inside his mind is drawing maps to a different world
from what we experience. That every time he gets stopped,
pinned, dropped and held down. That he won't understand
why…why the world…the world of the police…the world
of the authority who are meant to protect him. Supposed
to help him are stopping, searching and stripping him of
what dignity he has…cause everytime he leaves the flat…
every time he chases those pavements, my mind will be
chasing the thought of will I ever see him again?

Extended pause.

CAT   we can't keep him. We can't afford to keep him…cause
it's not that I don't love him, it's that I love him too much
to see him suffer… Be held back for the 2 things he can't
change…the two things that I wouldn't change about him.
But I can't afford to see him suffer…like so many men,
so many black mothers have suffered before. I refuse to
have my name stamped on a headline, with tears rolling
down my face, with my weave fucked up cause I ain't slept
in days. Days and weeks and years, resting on my heavy
shoulders stitching pain under my eyes reflecting to the
world the story of my dead son. Fuck it, I refuse to be a
static on a list of broken lives, broken boys, broken mothers.
I refuse to have his life mapped out like this… So what I'm
trying to say is…is…if you want to keep him. That's fine.
(Beat.) But I don't know if I can.

Tannoy: *Could Femi Oluwomi go to room 1*

End.

WOMB

by Somalia Seaton

...everyone
Bruvah
Josiah
Krums
Nah
Rah
Rolex
Sis
gonna
gotta
hench
wanna
ya

NKRUMAH

(M, late 20s). Afro-Caribbean British (Jamaica).
Board room charm, but don't run up on him.
South London but works in the city.
Master of switching 'it' on and off.

P. (PRISCILLA)

(F, early 30s). Afro-Caribbean British (Jamaica).
Fire. Easily riled. Passionate. Activist and teacher.

Notes:

Where lines appear within [ ] they are to be treated as lines
but not spoken.

Where ... appears at end of or beginning of lines
they suggest an overlapping in dialogue

Where ... appears within lines, it is to suggest
that the actor is finding their thoughts.

Where / appears within lines, that line is to be interrupted
by the following line

1.

That night.

Lights up on P, she addresses the crowd at a protest. In another space and time we see NKRUMAH, HE BREATHS HARD. HE IS TOPLESS. HE LOOKS DIRECTLY AT US.

A protest.

The crowd roars. P addresses us with a megaphone.

P

… And they were never held accountable. Their families were never given the justice they deserved. The press tried to paint the families as criminals, when they have repeatedly been victims to this so-called Empire. I don't even like that word. We are not victims. We are Kings and Queens, not a people that overcame slavery. Our history did not begin with slavery. We are glorious. Our sons and their future sons and our daughters will remember this moment in history, they will see how we rose together, they will see how Africans and Asians came together, how we rise together, how the white working class and the Polish immigrant, how all immigrants rose up together. We will fight until they hear us. There is no British Empire without the wealth of the nations from which you raped and stole from. Let us not forget Brothers and Sisters, This Great Empire taught Trump all he knows. Don't be distracted by his openly racist, xenophobic and sexist trash, It was this Empire, this Island, where marginalised peoples are still earning less than their white counterparts, it is this island that sent their missionaries to Africa to rape the land and our people. It is this Island that is responsible for the famine, the poverty the corruption that the media is familiar with on our great continent. You wanna talk about mass incarceration in the States, how African Americans are a minority yet make up the majority in their prisons, but it is the same thing here. Our men and our women make up a huge proportion of those locked up in psychiatric hospitals and prisons. Our women are offered drugs before talking therapies, our young boys are seen as a danger to society, beasts that need cages.

What has happened to Nkrumah is not uncommon, it is not new. Our resistance to the oppressions of this here land is what is new.

Now is the time, now we rise, now we turn to our brothers and sisters of different ethnicities, of different sexual orientations, of different faiths and beliefs and we will say, I am your keeper, I will fight for you! Together we are stronger! Together we will rise!

We will resist until they hear us! We resist until they hear us! We will resist until they hear us! Out of one came many, and together many will win.

211

2.

Time has passed.

We hear knocks on the door. It's barely lit, we just about make him out on the floor. The knocks grow more urgent.

A voice calls from outside.

P *(Cont'd.)*
I know you're in there

Knocks again.

I'll keep turning up until you let me in

Waits.
Fighting back tears.
Places a bag on the step.

P *(Cont'd.)*
I'm leaving some stuff here. I'll go but…don't let it go cold

She hesitates, then leaves.

3.

A week later. He sits, lifeless. She knocks again. A familiar routine. We hear her through the door.

P *(Cont'd.)*
Mum says she's been calling you. Says she's been dreaming 'bout you.

Waits.

P *(Cont'd.)*
Won't shut up 'bout how she's been praying, how the church has been praying. You've got every damn one of them praying to White Jesus in your honour! I hope you're happy.

He doesn't stir.
She waits.
He doesn't move.

P *(Cont'd.)*
She misses you Krums.
We all do.
… I love you

She leaves a bag on the step.

WOMB

4.

Weeks later.

We realise we've been in NKRUMAH's living room.

*P's been there for a while, though she stands like she's just arrived.
She holds a plastic bag. He sits on that same chair. He's surrounded
by weights.*

Awkwardness hangs for a while.

NKRUMAH
You gonna just…

P
Sorry
(Gesturing to the plastic bag she's gripping.)
Soup

NKRUMAH
Thanks

P
Red pea, and errmm I think some… Erm, curry goat and some tin stuff

NKRUMAH
Nice

P
Should still be warm

NKRUMAH
Cool

Beat.

P
She ain't
cookin'
like that for me

No reply.

You should call her /back…

NKRUMAH
You gonna take your coat off?

She does. Slowly hangs it. Watches him.

P
Sure

Breaks the silence.

NKRUMAH
I was…

Gestures to his weights.

P
She's just concerned…

NKRUMAH
(Ignoring her.) … It helps…

P
Krums.

NKRUMAH alternates between sit ups and press ups. She watches him. It's silent apart from his heavy breathing.

NKRUMAH
Hench
innit
?

She laughs.

P
Yeah, alright!

He continues.
She finds her words.

P *(Cont'd.)*
The lawyer's… [been calling]

No response.

P *(Cont'd.)*
Told them you've been back and forth at the hospital for check ups

NKRUMAH
I haven't

P
Right. Well thought it best I let them know you'll be in touch soon.

NKRUMAH bolts up.

NKRUMAH
You want a drink?

P
No. Thank you

WOMB

NKRUMAH
Sure?

P
I want to talk

NKRUMAH
Okay

P
I mean it

NKRUMAH
Okay

P
You asked for space I gave you space.
I'm on your side…

NKRUMAH
… Okay…

P
… I'm here to help…

NKRUMAH
… I'm good Sis…

P
… I know…

NKRUMAH
… Do you?

Beat.

P
Listen
We have well over fifty thousand signatures already…
Fifty thousand!
Are you hearing me?

NKRUMAH
Mmmhmm

P
There are people from across the globe reaching out to me daily,
wanting to help, begging to help

He stops his reps. Gathers himself.

If you're not feeling your lawyers, we'll get new ones, I've had five offer their services already, I've had people from all over the world offer their services, and now we have a website, it's... [even easier for people to get in touch]

NKRUMAH
You set up a website?

P
Well yeah...

NKRUMAH
For what?

P
What do you mean for what?/ To share information /obviously...

NKRUMAH
I mean for what?....
On what?

P
On all of it...

NKRUMAH
I told you though

P
Yes, but do you know how many cases there have been in the last ten years? How many families have been torn apart, communities / silenced because they think they'll lose...

NKRUMAH
Priscilla... Priscilla... I don't care about any of that

P
Do you know how many people have been paid off?

NKRUMAH
I don't care

P
It's important for people to know that they can press charges against the police and win.

NKRUMAH
You don't listen P

Beat.

P
It's bigger than / you...it's...

WOMB

NKRUMAH
This is my life.
Mine

P
Exactly

NKRUMAH
And I want it back

P
Exactly

NKRUMAH
No drama

P
I know that / but...

NKRUMAH
No you don't

P
I know you're scared

NKRUMAH
I'm not scared

P
We have support from all over the world Krums

NKRUMAH
What aren't you understanding?

P
Look I know how you feel

NKRUMAH
You don't know shit P, you're not hearing me 'cause you don't listen,
that's your problem, that's always been your problem. You talk too much

P
You haven't even let me...

NKRUMAH
... Everyone don't always wanna hear you speak, everyone don't
always wanna know what you have to say and what you fuckin think,
now I'm fuckin swearing, you got me fuckin swearing P, I don't swear
'round you and I'm fuckin swearing

P
Alright

NKRUMAH

It's not fuckin alright Priscilla! You won't let me be alright. I told you, I told all of you lot, I'm going back to work

P

And that's great Krums / It really is but...

NKRUMAH

You wanna just wipe away everything I've worked for, wanna prove something, open up our door, let the central heating out, let the whole world into our living room all up in our business, that's what you wanna do? And for what? To be connected with people, become some crusader for the masses? Fuck that

Beat.

P

Rah, poetic.

NKRUMAH

I don't want none of this

P

And I do?

NKRUMAH

Yeah

P

All my fault, yeah?

NKRUMAH

Nah, don't do that

P

But that's what you're saying

NKRUMAH

Again, you're not hearing me

P

I'm hearing you, Krums, loud and clear
I did this to you. I put you in that hospital bed, I made our Mother's hair turn the greyest grey, I made the foundations of our family, the stability of our family just mash up, me? I mashed it all up. I made you lock yourself up in this flat for months, not eating, not talking to nobody. I did this, yeah?

Beat.

NKRUMAH

I'm not you Priscilla

P
Right

Silence.

P *(Cont'd.)*
Josiah asked for you every single night before bed ya know. It's like
he knew. I stopped him going to all his favourite clubs, because it
was easier to take that away from him rather than listen to Mum
begging me not to leave him to walk home alone. Me, ya know,
scared. Can you imagine such a ting.

NKRUMAH
I was fine

P
You didn't see what we saw

NKRUMAH
And you never saw what I saw

Beat.

P
I can't get a drink, nah?

NKRUMAH
You said you didn't want one

P
Sometimes we say we don't want things and the people we love
know better

NKRUMAH
Yeah well. Kitchen ain't moved

P
Guests serves themselves now yeah?

NKRUMAH
Kitchen ain't moved

P
Neither have you

NKRUMAH
Apparently

P
Seems like you ain't moving nowhere Bruvah man...

NKRUMAH
Move in my own way... Move when I want to...

P

... Seems like you're lookin' to let this world crush your spirit Bruvah man...

NKRUMAH

... Said I move when I want to. Beat of my own drum...

P

... Seems like you don't need to hold my hand no more...

NKRUMAH

Never said...

P

Feels that way

NKRUMAH

It's not

P

Feels like you wanna dash me

NKRUMAH

Nah

P

Feels like you wanna dash all of us

NKRUMAH

No.

P

You're hiding

NKRUMAH

No

P

You're hiding behind your biceps, and your crisp shirts, your vintage Rolex, your cheap dates in the city, that ain't you. Where are you?

Silence.

P *(Cont'd.)*

There's a march on Saturday
For you
Well inspired by you, thousands of people asking them to open up your case. Your lawyers...

NKRUMAH

I don't have any lawyers

WOMB

P

Why are you doing this?

NKRUMAH

Why are you?

P

There is a march, scheduled in your honour.

NKRUMAH

Cancel it

P

People are rising together, collectively to fight back, and we are at the epicentre of that fire, we are driving it. What you went through will…

NKRUMAH

Will what? What I went through will what? Will never happen to another man, walking on the right side of the street, walking in the opposite direction. Doing the right thing, working harder than all of them, turning up, knowing how to speak how to walk how to maintain his position in the Matrix, it will never happen again? To another man like me, that feels the rage bubbling away in his stomach, yet he turns up, knows how to speak, knows how to walk, knows how to maintain. I can't worry about that. Do you understand me, I can't worry about none 'a that. I gotta turn up, be seen, be heard, path the way for the next ones, I don't have time to fight a system not designed for me to succeed overtly. I gotta show up, be seen be heard, get shit done, don't complain. Because I don't have time. None of us do. You wanna walk around with your face screw up, mash up the place and scream "please Sir some more" whilst you're doing it. You wanna ask for hand outs, you wanna demand recognition for your existence, from a country that has enslaved you like it enslaved your ancestors. You expect these people to give you respect whilst you're shouting them down. Nah, that can't run. You've gotta turn up, talk right, walk right and get on. Stop complaining. Stop demanding. Stop asking. You've gotta learn how they eat, how they breathe, how they love their women, their men, and you've gotta infiltrate from the inside. Not jump up and down outside the gates screaming "pick me."

You're a liability. You whine too much. You want freedom? Learn how to make them see themselves when they look at you, take it from the inside. I don't need to stand on no picket line, sis. I'm trying to survive. I need to survive. You think you're the only one that reads, the only one that knows the stats, the only one that knows that the image of me makes up the population inside those cages. Hospital cages, prison cages. I'm trying to survive. Let me survive.

*Another space and time we see NKRUMAH as we did at the start,
HE BREATHS HARD. HE IS TOPLESS HE IS BATTERED, HE LOOKS
DIRECTLY AT US.*

*He continues to get beaten. We see him flung from one space to
another, punched in the gut. His body flies through the space. If he
could get himself off of the floor he could make it. He tries. He fails.
He tries again. He fights someone. Punching and kicking and dodging
and diving. He charges from one part of this contained space, to
another, falling, getting back up again. He is in a bad way. He is
alone. He falls to the floor.*

*Simultaneously, lights up on P – Another space and time. She steps
forward. She is beaten down. She steps forward again. She is beaten
down. She steps forward again. Beaten. Steps forward. Beaten.
Steps forward. Keeps walking forward. Keeps walking forward.
Wraps arms around NKRUMAH.*

Lights fade down.

MANIFESTO

by Courttia Newland

A One-Act-Play

*A small **playground** area. Estate walls. **Swings**, a **Roundabout**, a **See-Saw** and **Walled Sandpit**. Four youths, all black, all hoodies, jeans and trainers sit in various places. They are of similar age, build and height. Their names denote the colour of their clothes:*

BLUE DREDD *sits on the ROUNDABOUT. He puffs on a SPLIFF, HOOD raised.*

RED DEE *leans against the SWINGS, removes dirt from his FINGERNAILS.*

GREY WOLF *sits on the SANDPIT WALL, drawing patterns with the toe of his NIKE.*

BLACK ATTACK *leans against the SEE-SAW, hands in his pockets, looking at the sky.*

– or –

*A black box space with three young men leant against walls. Doesn't matter who's where, as long as none are **BLACK**. He stands centre stage, facing the audience.*

Each youth is silent. They ignore each other, lost in thought.
BLACK *comes to, blinks, looks around. Steps forward, hands remain in pockets.*

BLACK I wanna hold the funeral.

All youths stop what they're doing, look.

BLACK *(Emphatic.)* I wanna hold the funeral. About time.

GREY It ain time.

BLUE *(Surprised.)* How you mean?

GREY It ain nearly time.

RED Tell him nuh!

GREY Time is running and running and passing, but it don't reach yet.

RED *(Shrugs.)* True story.

GREY Time is hard-eyed, death-cloaked Marine stepping into tomorrow with nuttin more than the price of power and violent pessimism, but he don't reach yet.

BLACK *kisses his teeth, turns.*

GREY's *warming up, stands.*

GREY Time's first light, a peek on the horizon, but he ain flood the sky. Time's a slow swelling belly, but the yout' ain come. Time's stiff, arthritic claws, gossamer hair and liver spots, but we ain pass last rites yet.

BLACK (*Holding up hands.*) All right, all right, allow me man! (*Beat.*) I'm still holdin the funeral.

RED Man ain hearin right...

BLACK You the ones ain heard. It's screamin, bellowin and moanin but you lot act like you're deaf. Front page obituaries blud, headline news. Tings dead fam. Done. Ting keel over and fall. No revivals, no reincarnation.

RED We need a revolution.

BLACK Think Tracy Chapman's gonna help! (*Laughs.*) Think she ever could? Ting's dead famo, truss!

RED We need silent talkers, mind walkers, buss man up with metaphysical spiritual head nods; I get you, whatever you say. We need speechers, preachers, long arm reachers, turn pockets and empty minds out on rough pavements, seekin to find... (*Shrugs.*) Us. I suppose.

BLACK Dreamer...

GREY Thank God for the dreamers.

BLACK (*Taunts, includes both.*) Hip Hop prophets!

RED At least we root for the dreamers. (*Walks over to GREY, touches his fist.*) Fuck the numbers, at least we didn't flop.

BLACK The numbers. Fuck. You. Yuh see me? The numbers fuck *us* and we all flop, all fall down like some nursery rhyme or should I put it in your terms, like a Kanye West hit, you know what I'm sayin homie? (*Reaches a hand out to GREY, who waves him off, BLACK laughing, not caring.*) Stats and projection epitaphs in dark ink designs that melt in your mind, not in your hands blud. (*Holds hands palms up.*) No evidence. No commonsense or karma. Killed that, crushed it. Or at least choked till it can't get up. Put a hold on long enough, it'll pass 'way eventually.

GREY Don't give in.

BLACK How you mean?

GREY A mirror held the wrong way bounces light direct in your eyes. It becomes difficult to see, painful. Held in that position too long, the subject risks a danger of retina dysfunction, blindness.

BLACK Man tinks he's smart.

GREY We've become refractions of our own nightmares. Wake up.

RED Wake up my brother.

BLACK *kisses his teeth, turns.*

BLACK I wanna hold the funeral, don't business...

RED This guy!

GREY Tell him fam. School him.

RED *steps up.*

RED You don't remember black smoke and thunder? Forty-two days and nights of slow entropy, sky turn blue, to white, to battleship grey? Don't remember streamers and news reports, pork pie hats and dark suits, shivered trepidation on docks? Don't remember razor bumped white skin, black boots with tarmac gleam, window signs that became reverberated clichés, an on-goin echo?

BLACK Yeah, yeah, yeah, done know...

BLACK *turns around.*

RED How bout thin brown branches ate by forest fire, a new cross raised in protest, 13 dead disciples? Police an thieves on street, young rebellion?

BLACK *doesn't answer. His back is turned, shoulders hunched. He's crying, but the boys don't know it.*

GREY Take man back fam. Way back.

RED Bruv. You don't remember ships in the night, a home we never knew; industrial necklaces with skin and bone beads, red, black and green fires, revolution? Don't remember Nanny, Tacky, Ngola Ann Nzinga, Sam Sharpe and Marcus Garvey, Massa's house, cane and cotton, rape and rotten food? *(Goes quiet.)* You forget where we *all* come from; you an me an dem too; streams of gold, temples, raised stones of 200 pyramids in Upper Kemit, Sudan to dem foreign man. Abundance, ancestors... What blud, you forgotten *us*?

BLACK *turns, has tears in his eyes, he's angry. Shouts.*

BLACK It's all those tings! Cos ah all dem tings its dead fam! Dat's what killed it innit? Guns and gold, diamonds and cassiterite, blood and bones and mucus of the long dead... Our fossils, fuel, everyting! Minerals and mishap, conquest and corruption, ripped from the flesh of our mother and man's tryin go on like I ain even got the sense to mourn that blud, man thinks I can turn away like it don't pain me! *(Beats chest.)* I weep for our mother blud! I bawl for the immortals! I give tanks for the blud she put in my veins, feed her body with fresh water and prayers, beat sterile concrete until she feels my fists! I dance so the ancestors see me and I'm gonna hold the funeral cos it's done blud, they killed it, the fuckin ting's dead!

*The boys are silent. No one looks at **BLACK**. **BLUE** raises his head.*

BLUE We need a manifesto.

BLACK *(Points at all three.)* Manifestyo…

BLUE What, man's taking the piss?

BLACK *(RP.)* I do not thumb my nose at you sir!

BLUE *gets to his feet, walks a few steps towards **BLACK**. It's a confrontation, a standoff.*

BLUE Are you dizzy blud?!

All three look up. Stare. Burst into simultaneous laughter. BLACK's is somewhat forced.

RED *(Still laughing.)* Speak bredrin.

BLUE We need to do more fam. Think more. Gameplan and rules. Get wise, you get me?

RED I get you.

GREY So what you sayin?

BLUE I dunno much.

RED Know enough.

BLACK *(Sarky.)* Say enough.

BLUE Man ain no intellectual.

BLACK *(Impatient.)* Speak man!

BLUE All right, all right, just makin man know…

GREY 'He who listens can hear…' You know dem ones?

RED Lay it down fam. Man know enough.

BLUE Cool. *(Looks around, gathers himself.)* Point one: Honour thy father and thy mother…

GREY True talk.

BLACK Standard…

RED Be specific blud. Break it down.

BLUE Remember the past.

GREY nods, satisfied.

GREY And the present. Mix 'em in safe spaces. Share us. A collective healing pool.

RED A time for reconnection.

BLACK Recharge, rebuild.

BLUE We need a day.

GREY We gotta month.

All four simultaneously kiss their teeth.

RED FUBU.

BLUE Damn right. For us, by us.

BLACK So BHM can KMBA.

*All laugh. **RED** smiles.*

RED So what day?

GREY Garvey's birthday!

BLUE Emancipation day.

BLACK What, we don't have no traditional dates? Thought we was tryin to remember?

BLUE Who knows one? You?

BLACK shrugs, looks down.

BLUE We need a date, common consensus.

GREY Damn right. Across the whole diaspora.

BLACK Good luck.

Silence.

RED What's point two?

BLUE More griots, storytellers.

ALL Yeah.

GREY Tell the world who we are.

RED Tell ourselves.

BLACK Got nuff already…

MANIFESTO

GREY True talk; all the poets and ancestors.

RED MC's and writers.

BLUE Maybe point two is; *acknowledge* our griots and storytellers.

BLACK Feelin that.

BLUE Point three. Re-education.

Youths perk up.

RED Like, how?

BLUE Programs.

GREY Schools.

BLACK's shaking his head.

RED What happened to the schools we got?

BLACK Are you nuts?

RED The responsibility's theirs. Right?

BLACK Won't teach us to defend ourselves.

RED Course man.

BLACK Survival of the fit, hunter don't train prey.

RED Our rights make it right. We pay taxes.

GREY *Whole* other story.

BLACK Taxes never fund empowerment.

BLUE Why not?

RED Pay ourselves. Go independent.

GREY Used to be weekend schools.

BLUE And they was ram.

RED How you know?

BLUE Dad showed me innit…

GREY Big up La Rose. Critchlow.

BLUE We still got programs. Big up Gus John.

ALL *(Murmur in unison like a prayer, as if saying 'Amen'.)* Big up.

BLUE Revisionist history, our schools or theirs. Don't business which.

ALL murmur agreement.

GREY That's a whole other convo. I waan go home at some point. Kiss the wife…

They others smile knowingly, swap looks.

BLUE Point four. Economic strength.

RED We got Cosby!

All laugh.

BLUE *(Imitates Cosby.)* Come on people!

All laugh harder.

BLACK Dunno about my man…

BLUE Say nuttin, he might sue yuh arse…

GREY We got Oprah!

BLUE Who's dis we? America?

BLACK We can't claim none ah dem man bruv.

RED All right, all right, we got plenty business man.

BLACK Name one.

GREY The man who owns Gatwick airport. A brudda.

BLACK He don't own that shit.

GREY Bankers and music man, ballers for big leagues, sisters working FTSE's on the Wharf.

RED He's talking 'bout a nation. Individual wealth can't run.

BLUE We got a nation. Our mothers. Her sons an daughters. Collective resources.

BLACK Call that strength?

GREY In numbers.

BLUE Call it mindset. Say it's strength, it is. Call it weak, it is.

RED Every mickle makes a mockle…

BLACK Until I spend mockles like dollars I'll keep my excitement to myself.

BLUE Bruv. We all know how to spend, but how to share, retain? Money in our pockets should stay there.

MANIFESTO

BLACK To do what?

RED Our businesses.

GREY Our banks.

BLACK Do we even have a bank?

They look at each other. BLACK kisses his teeth.

GREY Build one.

BLACK's growing agitated and beginning to fume, pacing on the spot, jittery and impatient. RED notices.

RED Come man, next ting.

BLUE We need a leader.

All three wince, draw breath. BLACK stops pacing, regains attention.

BLACK Touchy.

BLUE *(Smiling.)* But we need him.

GREY Or her. Remember Nanny? Nzinga?

RED We got Obama.

They wince.

RED Healthcare and gays in the military! *(Quick look at the others.)* Not that I bat or nuttin, but I kinna like socialism…

GREY Socialism's the African way.

BLUE He ain ours. I hear you, but we still need a leader.

BLACK *(Snide.)* Preferably one that don't bomb dark people.

RED I miss Huey…

GREY Malcolm…

BLUE Dem man are in the wind. Can't see dem. System cut cane.

BLACK They weren't ours either.

GREY They're everyone's.

RED Diaspora over nationalism.

BLACK Someone who speaks for *us* fam. It's not Golden Ratio.

GREY No politicians.

RED Bare activists in the hood.

BLACK But who's got the power?

RED Blud, this ain He-Man.

BLUE and GREY laugh.

BLACK You think this is funny?

GREY Can't name one.

RED Maybe it's collective.

BLUE So who we got? Collectively?

Silence.

RED We need a leader.

Silence.

BLUE Point 6. Politically aware artists.

GREY and RED nod hard, BLACK smiles grimly and shakes his head.

BLUE What now?

BLACK Beyonce at the Super Bowl, yeah?

GREY She get ban from Capital?

BLUE Welcome to the struggle my sister!

RED He means on tracks, or for real?

BLUE What d'you think?

GREY *(Spits lyric, RED joins in halfway through.)* 'Guru told me slow up the flow, cos science and metaphor will slow up the dough.' *(Beat, all nod.)* Big up Lowkey, Kweli, Akala, MCD…

RED *(Jumps in.)* Big up Badu, Monae, Rhapsody…

All make gun signs with their fingers, point in the air.

ALL BRA…!

Stop. Look at each other.

GREY See what we almost did there?

RED *(Raps, deep voice.)* 'Psychological enslavement, is the arrangement…'

BLUE That's what I'm saying, it runs deep, man has to keep checkin yourself.

MANIFESTO

GREY Roll off the last few I beg you. I'm gettin that itchy, need-to-see-the-missus feelin...

BLUE laughs, stands tall, from this point on the others start speaking over him and the scene begins to grow more chaotic as BLUE tries to make his point to a disinterested audience.

BLUE Alright, point 7; honour our women.

BLACK We need a manifesto fuh dat?

GREY That's what I'm tryina do innit, honour my women properly. I waan go home an honour her right now...

RED For real bruv, certain man need reminding. Don't see the gyalist is a modern day buck. Trauma affects those closest to the victim. Can't see horizon or sun.

GREY It start with family. Take care ah the home and the home takes care of the community, you get what I'm saying?

BLACK *(Vex, not listening to GREY.)* No power in victimhood fam.

BLUE *(Quickly.)* Point 8, cherish our sons and daughters; raise them right, never resent them.

RED When last you see your dad then?

BLACK *(Vex, snaps.)* This morning. At breakfast. Don't try it.

GREY My dad make sure I know how to be a good father so I'm teaching my yout, you know how? Love fam. Not patriarchal aggression, hugs and a solid relationship. *(Beat, looks at the others.)* He can box though, don't think he can't defend himself still...

BLACK *(Staring at RED.)* Joker.

RED Safe man, don't get vex; point taken.

BLACK You think the Black father's a myth? Invisible like Ether? You think we don't believe in raising our kids?

RED More than anyone else? Nah. But slavery and the migrant experience cleaved the family unit.

GREY My unit's strong king! I wanned a football team innit, but after the first two I change my mind quick.

RED and BLACK finally hear what GREY's saying and shoot him a confused look. Then continue.

BLACK If we got no self-belief, what's the point of a manifesto?

BLUE *(Loud, trying to maintain order.)* Point 9 *(Beat.)* disengage from class and skin-based hierarchy.

GREY *(To BLACK.)* We're human fam, not Gods and angels. Come from the heavens but land on earth just like everyone else. Not perfection, not enlightened, not evil.

RED Human being means being flawed, accepting flaws, loving them. Acceptance, not exceptional.

BLACK I'm saying inspirational. Truthful. Reality of existence, not the fantasy of the lost.

BLUE *(Loudest.)* Point 10 *(Beat, Blue sighs.)* Unity.

They stand and think. Black's still pissed, frowning, looks at them all in disbelief. They stare back, gauging the distance between each other.

BLACK *Now* you see why I wanna hold the funeral?

Beat.

RED It ain dead fam. Dormant.

GREY Comatose.

BLUE We keep it alive. Make it breathe. *(Beat.)* It needs us.

GREY Us

RED Us

RED, BLUE and GREY slowly look towards the audience, turn their bodies that way, stand rigid. BLACK steps off to one side, shaking his head.

BLUE It needs you.

GREY You.

RED You.

BLUE It needs we.

The three youths look towards the audience while BLACK continues shaking his head, looks at the floor. Lights down.

The End.

RUNNIN'

by Luke Reece

BRO and SIS are running. They are not speaking to each other.

BRO   Runnin' Runnin' and Runnin' Runnin'

BRO and SIS   and Runnin' Runnin' and Runnin' Runnin'
                  and Runnin' Runnin' and Runnin' Runnin'
                  and Runnin' Runnin' and Runnin' Runnin' and

SIS   The Black Eyed Peas!

BRO   I was on the cross-country team in elementary
                  school – except not on really because I never got
                  to compete against other schools. I just competed
                  to be the team. This new kid, this Asian kid just
                  shows me up, out of nowhere, like a week before
                  the school race, and he beats me. He gets put at
                  table group for to show around, and he beats me.
                  He is the only other coloured dude in my class, and
                  he beats me. Like, that's not cool. I was one place
                  off from making the team. He took my place.

SIS   The song is called 'Let's Get Retarded'
                  but they changed it to 'Let's Get it Started' for
                  obvious reasons.

BRO   My school made a slide show of the race and used
                  that song.

SIS   You can still listen to the original on Spotify
                  though. I think that's weird.

*SIS continues to say Runnin' Runnin' under her breath while BRO is
speaking.*

BRO   In the slide show there are pictures of everyone
                  starting the race, and everyone finishing the race.
                  I look so defeated.
                  He doesn't even care. Now I can only think of this
                  Asian kid when I hear the song. I used to like the
                  song.

SIS   We ate black-eyed peas with rice at family
                  dinners. I knew that it was the same as the music
                  group, but my brother didn't know.
                  Like, he had no idea.

BRO   No shit?

*They stop running and are now mid-water break, speaking to each
other.*

SIS	Yeah, we ate those all the time.
BRO	I ate Fergie.
SIS	Don't say that.
BRO	Will. I. Am. so sorry for putting ketchup on you.
SIS	Those are the shorts I got you for Christmas eh?
BRO	Mmhm.
SIS	They good?
BRO	Yeah, Lulu knows what she's doing. They're expensive for a reason.
SIS	Perks of working there – they were actually pretty cheap.
BRO	Wow, thanks sis.
SIS	Relatively speaking!
BRO	Next year don't expect anything nice okay?
SIS	Well you won't be getting anymore Lulu – I quit.
BRO	Why? You're due for a promotion like any day now. You run that place.
SIS	No, I don't run it.
BRO	You should.
SIS	I can't.
BRO	You don't want to?
SIS	I just can't, I'm not meant to – I don't know.
BRO	What happened?
SIS	They promoted someone else. This new girl – white girl – Brittany.
BRO	Does she have more experience or someth –
SIS	No. It's cool, I'm fine.
BRO	I mean you quit so clearly –
SIS	Come on, that's a long enough break, let's get going.

BRO and SIS are running. They are not speaking to each other.

RUNNIN'

BRO　　　　Runnin' Runnin' and Runnin' Runnin' and

SIS　　　　When I was six, I was put in this six-year-old race,
　　　　　　　for six-year-olds, at our father's work picnic. He
　　　　　　　finished first in the dad race, my brother finished
　　　　　　　2nd in the nine-year-old race annnd I finished 3rd
　　　　　　　in the six-year-old race. It was pretty cool. There's
　　　　　　　a photo of us all together, standing in order with
　　　　　　　our ribbons.

*SIS continues to say Runnin' Runnin under her breath while BRO
speaks.*

BRO　　　　Dad ALWAYS finished first – every year.
　　　　　　　It was ridiculous. The other families would joke
　　　　　　　about it with him – "Are you taking the race again
　　　　　　　this year? Nobody's fast like you!"
　　　　　　　I wanted to be fast like him. Playing manhunt
　　　　　　　at school I won like 90% of the time. In soccer
　　　　　　　– fastest guy on the field, no question – always
　　　　　　　running.

A white male STRANGER is jogging in the opposite direction.

BRO and SIS　Runnin' Runnin' and Runnin' Runnin' and Runnin'
　　　　　　　Runnin' and Runnin' Runnin' and Runnin' Runnin'
　　　　　　　and Runnin' Runnin' and Runnin' Runnin' and
　　　　　　　Runnin' Runnin' and

STRANGER　Runnin' from the cops?

BRO　　　　Uh.

SIS　　　　What?

*SIS stops, turns around, and jogs to catch up with the STRANGER.
She trips him. BRO is still running.*

STRANGER　What the fuck?

BRO　　　　Runnin' Runnin'

SIS　　　　What did you just say?

STRANGER　I said what the fuck?

SIS　　　　No, before that.

STRANGER　You're crazy I didn't say anything.

SIS　　　　I heard it.

BRO　　　　Sis?

BRO turns and runs back towards them. SIS kicks STRANGER.

STRANGER   Bitch get the fuck away from me, I didn't say shit.

SIS   You said something as you ran passed us.

BRO   Sis you okay?

STRANGER   You're sister's a crazy ass bitch.

BRO   Don't you —

STRANGER begins to get up, SIS kicks him again and then grabs the collar of his shirt and pins him to the ground. He spits in her face. She punches him. BRO is frozen in shock. She punches him again.

SIS   You asked us if we were running from the cops.

She punches him again.

SIS   You think you're funny, you think this is a joke. It's so easy for you to do that, to just run by and say something in passing without any consequences. It means nothing to you but it's my life, it's our life. I don't deserve to be treated this way. I deserve better. I deserve a fucking promotion…in life.

STRANGER pushes SIS off of him. BRO stands between SIS and the STRANGER. STRANGER walks towards BRO.

STRANGER   This — this kind of behavior is the kind of fucking shit I expect from —

BRO swings and misses, STRANGER punches BRO, BRO punches back. An ASIAN MAN is jogging by, sees what's happening and immediately restrains STRANGER.

ASIAN MAN   Go!

STRANGER   What the fuck? Get off me! These little shits are —

ASIAN MAN   Why don't you shut up?

STRANGER   What are you doing man leave me alone this has nothing to do with you.

ASIAN MAN   Ha.

SIS   You don't have to —

BRO   Thank you.

RUNNIN'

STRANGER	I swear I'm gonna call the cops! I was just defending myself.
ASIAN MAN	The only witness says otherwise.
STRANGER	That's not fair, that's bullshit!
SIS	Exactly.
BRO	Exactly...
ASIAN MAN	You two go. It's okay.
STRANGER	Yeah just fucking run off then! Fucking cowards.
BRO	Come on.
SIS	*(To STRANGER.)* You listen to me before we run, before we run off like we've been doing for so long. Running, and resisting the urge to beat you to a pulp, refusing to be bruised by your words – that's not the act of a coward. Remember that. It takes a lot of strength to put up with ignorant people like you every goddamn day.
BRO	Let's go.

BRO & SIS run.

BRO and SIS	Runnin' Runnin' and Runnin' Runnin' and Runnin' Runnin' and Runnin' Runnin' and Runnin' Runnin' and Runnin' Runnin' and Runnin' Runnin' and Runnin' Runnin' and Runnin' Runnin' and

End.

THEY

by Tawiah BenEben M'Carthy

CHARACTER They are walking on opposite ends of the room, walking on a straight line up and down the stage. Praying in tongues, fervently, the prayers get louder and louder, they stop abruptly and turn to face the audience short of breath.

YOU For those of you who might not be aware,

I Might not know…

YOU THEY are dead.

I Yes

YOU Passed away unexpectedly in the night.

I In their sleep.

YOU Yes.

I THEY left behind OTHERS

YOU Yes. Husbands,

I Wives,

YOU Sons, Daughters…

I Yes, the poor children

YOU Yes, poor THEM.

I How sad?

YOU Yes, very sad.

I They are too young to be without./How will they survive this/ yes, living/when death keeps cheating at the game, knowing we are born to die. ??????????

YOU Them.
Life?
Yes.
THEY were too young to die.

I Yes, and how very sad.

CHARACTER They begin walking up and down the stage again. Praying silently. They stop abruptly.

I What will you say?

YOU when?

I when we are asked where we were

YOU They will ask where we were

I Where were we, when They died?

CHARACTER You left and after some time I left. They were asleep. I went down and slept, to rest. You left so I left.

YOU It had been a long day, walking there to there. I needed some time, by myself.

I There was a thirst, I had to quench. I left, but only for a time

CHARACTER You left so I left

YOU and I and now THEY are dead

YOU And WE are here.

I We cannot wear WHITE,

YOU there are no celebrations here,

I our BLACKs no longer fit.

YOU They were too young to died.

I For those of you who might not know, THEY, died last night.

YOU They were too young to die

I They passed in their sleep,

YOU alone.

I They left behind others.

YOU and I We wear RED.

YOU This time we wear RED.

YOU and I There is only danger.

YOU So WE wear RED

I within our eyes and on our bodies.

CHARACTER THEY run across the stage. THEY raise their hands up in unison as in worship, fall to their knees and continue to pray in tongues, the prayer turns into clapping, worship. They stop abruptly, walk to each other center stage and stand side by side.

I For those of you who might not know, We are here.

YOU We were here before yesterday and the days before.

I I was here and then you came after me and now we are here as us.

YOU for those of you, who might not know…

THEY

I Might not be aware

YOU We were here when They were born

I I wore white

YOU I wore white

I we wore white to celebrate when They were born. We were here.

YOU Here as us.

I They came with others,

YOU With wives and husbands

I holding hands

YOU sons and daughter

I fist in air, chanting words

YOU They took to the streets,

I fist in the air, singing songs

YOU For those of you that might not know

I They

KEEP SAFE

by Kanika Ambrose

stage directions are meant to be spoken along with the action

*She holds her black man as close as she can. She envelopes
her black man as close as she can. She entangles herself in,
encapsulates her black man as close as she can.*

WOM'N They say no charges will come to "subject officer"
who shot Andrew Loku but we still want answers.
I saw Andrew Loku and I saw my...

MAY'N You don't have to...

WOM'N Shot in the chest. Right here.

*She puts her head on his heart. She undoes his shirt, undoes her
shirt and puts her heart to his heart.*

That's what we want.

If something breaks in our home, don't go outside
with a hammer to fix it. Somebody might see you
and call the cops cuz' they feel threatened and the
cops come and they call you but you don't hear
them 'cuz you get so focused when you're fixing
things. You get so focused on simple things. You
get so focused on what's at hand and finishing
it that you can't split your focus and I can't even
think of loosing you for not being able to split your
focus between a cop and a broken...

*MAY'N wears a red cap, vest and a little porch light and holds out
his arm. For a moment.*

Don't they know this is our house? You worked
double shifts for a whole year to afford it.
But a neighbour may not recognize you because
you're hardly ever home because
you work so hard and so long just so you can have
one day to fix things in front of your house with a
hammer if you need to.

And we're seen as anti-social because when we
get home we're tired from having had to work
twice as hard to get where we got while the stay
at home mom creepin' out her window might see
you with a hammer and see you as a threat.

Be safe today.

You better not drive the BMW.

MAY'N Why not?

WOM'N   Because everybody knows that the only way a
              black man can be driving a luxury car is if he's
              doing something illegal.

MAY'N   Like working in the fish market?

WOM'N   Like taking too long. If the cops come and ask
              you for your license, even if you try to be good
              and say "yes sir" and don't ask why and you look
              in your glove compartment and you take too long
              looking in your glove compartment they might
              feel threatened. Especially if it's a little white lady
              cop with a black belt and military style training,
              who lifts twice your body weight before breakfast.
              She may feel threatened by you because you're
              taking too long to pull your I.D. from your glove
              compartment and you, who I have to force to use
              hand weights once a week, you, with your winter
              pot belly, you know what little pudgy black men can
              do to little shiny white things right Carolyn Bryant?

MAY'N   Damn.

WOM'N   Plus you're Jamaican.

MAY'N   Damn.

WOM'N   Everybody knows that Jamaicans are the worst
              black people of all.

MAY'N   Damn

WOM'N   Find a Jamaican man, kill him on the spot. I just –

MAY'N   We used to see that every weekday

WOM'N   After work

MAY'N   At 6 o'clock

WOM'N   Watching the news and praying it's not another
              black man.

MAY'N   And especially not a Jamaican.

              Are you really that scared? Nothing is going to
              happen to me. I leave here at the same time every
              day. I kiss you on your face; pull my side of the
              covers back over you. I make my coffee and I drive
              to work. I do that, I come back home. I've always
              been an excellent husband, father and friend.

KEEP SAFE

	I play basketball on the weekends and I give back to my community by volunteering at my local boys and girls club. I love my mama and –
WOM'N	You go to church
MAY'N	I go to church
WOM'N	Every Sunday
MAY'N	I go to church
WOM'N	With your mama
MAY'N	Church.
WOM'N	Breaks into loud church lady tears.

AAAAAAAAAAOOOOOOOOWWW! Why'd they take my baby from me, why'd they take my baby from me? My son was a good boy. He never got into no trouble. He was always in church.

| **MAY'N** | dressed as a church lady |

Always in church.

| **WOM'N** | And he never disrespected his mama. |
| **MAY'N** | He was a good boy. |

She drops her church lady persona and looks at her man.
She takes off his church lady persona and looks at her man.
She takes his face into her hands and kisses him and she…

She holds her black man as close as she can. She envelopes her black man as close as she can. She entangles herself in, encapsulates her black man as close as she can.

| **WOM'N** | I grew up with two brothers. Either one of them could have been Jermiane Carby. Especially the younger one, he had an attitude on him. I used to go to bed at 9 o'clock and be in my room with my head to the wall waiting to hear him open his bedroom door and sink into his bed dirty clothes and all. I used to be frightened to see him come home with a scarf on his head, frightened to see him bring home any friends dressed in "thug wear" frightened that one day there would be no more of him, and for no reason and no one would care so at least, don't wear a sweater today okay? |

4 STUDENTS

by Jordan Laffrenier

4 students sit at their desks in an old style classroom. They are sporting school uniforms: black ties, white dress shirts & dark dress pants. They stand when they speak. Student #4 is a white male, all of the other students are black any gender.

SCENE 1. LANGSTON HUGHES.

STUDENT #3
Theme for English B by Langston Hughes

STUDENT #1
The instructor said

STUDENT #4
Go home and write
a page tonight
and let that page come out of you
Then, it will be true.

STUDENT #1
I wonder if it's that simple

STUDENT #2
I am twenty-two

STUDENT #3
Colored

STUDENT #1
born in Winston-Salem

STUDENT #3
I went to school there

STUDENT #1
Then Durham

STUDENT #2
Then here to this college on the hill above Harlem.

STUDENT #1
I am the only coloured student in my class

STUDENT #1 and STUDENT #2
I am the only coloured student in my class

STUDENT #1
The steps from the hill lead down into Harlem,
through a park,

STUDENT #2
then I cross St. Nicholas,

STUDENT #3
Eighth Avenue, Seventh, and I come to the Y,

STUDENT #1
the Harlem Branch Y, where I take the elevator
up to my room, sit down, and write this page:

STUDENT #2
and write this page

STUDENT #3
and write this page:
It's not easy to know what is true for you or me
at twenty-two, my age. But I guess I'm what
I feel and see and hear, Harlem, I hear you.
hear you, hear me – we two – you, me, talk on this page.
(I hear New York, too.) Me – who?

STUDENT #1
Me who?

STUDENT #2
Me – who?
Well, I like to eat, sleep, drink, and be in love.
I like to work, read, learn, and understand life.
I like a pipe for a Christmas present,
or records – Bessie, bop, or Bach.
I guess being colored doesn't make me **not** like
the same things other folks like who are other races.
So will my page be colored that I write?
Being me, it will not be white.

STUDENT #1
But it will be
a part of you, instructor.
You are white –
yet a part of me, as I am a part of you.
That's American.

STUDENT #2
Sometimes perhaps you don't want to be a part of me.
Nor do I often want to be a part of you.
But we are, that's true!
As I learn from you,
I guess you learn from me –
although you're older – and white –
and somewhat more free.
This is my page for English B.

SCENE 2. STUDENT #1

STUDENT #1
This is my page for English B
(hashtag) is an ethnic group; i imagine one self–
% (percent) is a type of clean water–
*(asterisk) is a crystalline solid material whose constituents
(atoms, molecules, ions) are arranged in a highly ordered
microscopic structure; **yes**, I just took that from the internet.
_(underscore) is my father. falling. failing. dying. how much does
the coffin of failed parent weigh?
^ (circumflex) is a visual perception – downwards – like the lower
half of the fridge holds a lower class painting I drew of my lower
life family, when I only knew letters in the lowercase.
, comma has evolved from virgule \ or backslash \. But no one
knows where backslash came from. In early editions of the bible
does it read that God created heaven and the earth and backslash.
Adam and Eve and Backslash. Or did it come from a falling dream,
a waking nightmare: . Baby what do you think when I wake up the
night screaming backslash. BACK SLASH. BACK SLASH. As if
the slash they left on his back is still bleeding, and even though
you are right next to me, baby I have never felt more alone.
| Vertical bar how do you stand so tall after the shin splints,
after the sunburn, after too many nights outs, after too many
nights in, after too much yeast and waste. Do you ever even
imagine collapsing. So much depends on you vertical bar.
So much depends on you.
Generic Currency will you ever remove yourself from corporate
imperialism. You are the 1% that people are mad at. You are a
Mcdonald's burger eating Beyonce in a Starbucks commercial.
When I ask you for change, I can not believe you have the decency
to walk on by. I hope you cut your pale white forehead on their red
red diamonds and your red red blood freezes into a noose.

Spacebar you are probably quite unconscious of forming phosphorescent delicate roads between structures. I have never seen myself on these angelic highways but I know they exist. This is why I remind myself, daily, that March 12th 2014 7:06 am is my time to die. I want to drown but I know I don't get to choose these things. I want to drown but I know I don't get to choose these things. I want to drown but I know I don't get to choose these things. I want to drown but I know I don't get to choose these things.

Quotation Marks you sick. ignorant. fuck. I know you wouldn't believe me if I said 'somedays I feel myself melting into the sky' as if the colours on my skin are fading, and I am screaming, no coloured lives matter. **I am fading. No coloured lives matter.**
ampersand I am fading.
ampersand I am fading.
ampersand I am fading.
ampersand I am fading. period.

SCENE 2. STUDENT #2

STUDENT #2
This is my theme for English B
I am sorry, I did not get the homework done again today, teacher.
No. Yes. I am sorry.
I have been struggling, I haven't had the time, and at home –
No, it's not my mom –
Please don't put me on the spot or I wont put my hand up anymore.
You put nobody on the spot 'cept me and that's not fair.
Mom says **you** are **racist**.
She said she had a teacher that was really mean to her, used to put her desk in a closet, made her work there. Failed her in all her classes. Mom used to cry deep tears. But I don't like that,
I just think you are real mean.
No, I am not trying to offend you.
No, the principal's office is not for me.
Yes, I know teachers work real hard.
But Teacher, I just don't think…you think…about me.

(Beat.)

I am real hungry, I can't think. Just give me more time
and I'll have something to present to you.
Something about my brother.

SCENE 3. STUDENT #4

STUDENT #4
This is my Theme for English B.
Most days I wish I were black so I had more to write about:
Pen in one hand, 600 years of oppression in the other:
I would aim the pen at the page and boom: words and letters, words and mother fucking letters!
There would be so much oppression in my life: women clutching their purses as I step on the bus; men clutching their son's hand tightly as I walk by mumbling in anger something like "we got to hurry up" or if they are really racist "we got to get to the other side of the street quick before that negro gets us", employers clutching Tom's resume tighter than mine because I would have a name like Trayvon and names like Trayvon scare white people.
I would have a gurl friend from somewhere exotic and dangerous like Washington Heights or Jamaica town or Queen and Sherbourne. She would speak in a thick Caribbean accent and that accent would show up in my work and that accent would make my work more interesting: because audiences love characters with accents it gives them something to write about.
I know so much about being black. I would never say it but I know more about being black then most of my black friends. But most days I feel like I do.

SCENE 4. STUDENT #3

STUDENT #3
This is my theme for English B
You are in your room
on your bed
back against your headboard
sharing a glass of wine
with Facebook
You are contemplating the hash tag
all lives matter thoughts prompted by a
 status about Food Choices
"All lives matter remember to eat right"
132 likes.
You comment.
0 likes.
I worry being black isn't cool anymore
I worry she'll leave me for someone cooler
I worry I am bigger than I am

bigger penis, bigger hands, bigger condoms, bigger chains
I worry I have been silent too long
& have given too many people too many opportunities to speak for me
I worry I don't look black enough or white enough:
that my lack of shade has created a lack of tribe
I worry they'll take away his body
I worry I'm next

SCENE 5. END OF CLASS

STUDENT #1
There are some things we know to be true:
1. Not all bees can sting. Male bees cannot.

STUDENT #2
2. Bee stings are acidic while wasp stings are alkaline.

STUDENT #3
3. The only letter that does not appear on the periodic table is J.
Bees have no concept of the periodic table or the letter J...
or do they?

STUDENT #4
Whites in the U.S. have more reported cases of bee sting related
injuries than blacks in the U.S

STUDENT #1
6. My chances of losing my body to police brutality are higher than
the chances of losing my body to a bee sting

STUDENT #4
7. I am the only white student in my class.

STUDENT #2
9.There are now more blacks in prison than there were blacks in
slavery. 1/3 Black males in the U.S will go to prison at some point
in their life times.

STUDENT #4
Many of these prison sentences are due to racist policing policies
set up by Bill Clinton that he later apologized for.

STUDENT #2
Me losing my body to a racist prison system is higher than losing
my body to a bee sting.

4 STUDENTS

STUDENT #3
No studies have been done comparing the violence of black people to the violence of bees.It has been proven that blacks are no more prone to violence than whites. In that way, we are equal.

HOW I SOMETIMES SURVIVE
by Meghan Swaby

Notes: The first lines from **The Most Dangerous Woman on the Subway** is from Kanye West's song "We Don't Care".

Page 3 **The Most Dangerous Woman on the Subway** line is from Kendrick Lamar's "Alright"

PART ONE

Toronto.
5:59pm Evening Rush Hour on a TTC Subway.
Commuter #1, Commuter #2 and
The Most Dangerous Woman on the Subway

The Most Dangerous Woman on the Subway

Throw your hands up in the sky

*Cause **we don't care what people say***

Commuter #1

I'm the person on the subway, crammed ass packed with people, grumpy hungry on my way home, pretending to be on my phone.

Tired, exhausted, scrolling

Tired, exhausted, scrolling

Another one shot – angry emoji

Tired, exhausted, scrolling

Peel police arrest a six-year-old black girl – sad emoji

Commuter #2

Tired, exhausted, scrolling

Black youth "accidently raped" by police in Paris – angry emoji

Tired, exhausted, scrolling

Another one shot – angry emoji

Commuter #2

White Terrorist kills six Muslim men while they pray – angry emoji

Tired, exhausted, scrolling

Commuter #1

Scrolling rolling eyes glazed over mind glazed over heart glazed over

Trying not to make eye contact with the wild girl in the corner

She is interfering with my –

Commuter #2

Tired, exhausted, scrolling

HOW I SOMETIMES SURVIVE

Commuter #1

But it's hard not to stare. She's moving so hard that people politely inch away

She keeps moving and smiling

She is singing to herself with her arms wide open

She is dark and dangerous her movements are limitless

She has no fear.

Commuter #2

She doesn't need music in her ears to dance. She pulses and taps and dabs and pops

She jerks and shake and glides through angry commuters.

Commuter #1

She is dancing...on the subway...during rush hour and we all hate her because she has a smile on her face and isn't sorry

She isn't tired,

She isn't exhausted

She isn't sorry

The Most Dangerous Woman on the Subway

Dancing as a fuck you to the feeling I woke up with this morning

Dancing because the only way you'll like this body dancing in public is to make you

Laugh

Smile

Wet

Hard

or clap.

This dance is for me and me only.

The Most Dangerous Woman on the Subway

This northbound party is making me cuck my foot up on a stroller and wine down past the seats down to the spilled coffee.

This is my Mas, my fete, my caribana, my j'ouvert, my jump up get'n on bad

because I don't know what else to do.

When you lose yourself in bashment the world stops and I just need things to stop for one second. We just need things to stop for one second because when I stop dancing lava will pour out my nose, I'll bleed fire and exhale smoke.

And I don't want to blow everyone up so I'm going to keep this up.

I'll keep dancing until my destination because my heart is so hot and cracked.

My heart is so hot and cracked.

Isn't your heart so hot and cracked?

The Most Dangerous Woman on the Subway

When I wake up every morning, I need to drink three liters of water just to start the day

I do my stretches drink my coffee make myself some toast and move

I don't stop till the sun comes down. I refuse to stop moving.
My muscles get sore and my feet calloused up over bunions aside

I wear this bouncing burning sweaty cracked black body with pride

(To audience.)

What is the song that makes you go "Ooh"? A song that makes you go "that's my JAAAAAM!"

As **The Most Dangerous Woman on the Subway** asks someone from the audience for their favorite song. If for some reason if no one from the audience suggests one, the **Most Dangerous Woman on the Subway** will offer one to the audience and try to get them dancing (however small).

<u>The Most Dangerous Woman on the Subway</u>

....I'm at the preacher's door

My knees gettin' weak and my gun might blow but we gon' be alright.

PART TWO
Here. Now
The following passage is
read from all "actors".
Some lines are spoken
together others not.
No one is the same
"character" from part one.
Everyone is themselves.

Together they read *"a litany for survival by audre lorde"*.

Blackout.

LETTERS TO A LOST FRIEND

by Mary Ann Anane

MILA

Black, 20

MISH (MICHELLE)

Asian, 20

Setting/Time: 2015. A dorm room.

A dark dorm bedroom with a lamp as the source of light. MISH opens the door. MILA enters cautiously, not looking MISH in the eye.

MISH
Do you want something to drink?

MILA
What?

MISH
Water?

MILA
Since when do you offer water to people?

MISH
I don't know. It's a gesture.

MILA
Don't make gestures. It's nice but –

MISH
Fine.

MILA
this isn't a nice thing…moment…whatever.

MISH
You ignored me yesterday.

MILA
I wasn't ready to talk to you.

MISH
Okay. That's fine.

Silence as MILA sits on MISH's bed.

MISH
But –

MILA
Oh / my god.

MISH
You ignoring me in public is awkward and everyone was staring at me. It was mean of you.

MILA
WHAT YOU DID WAS REALLY FUCKING SHITTY!
How do you not get that? Why do I have to explain that to you? Are you five?

MISH
No. You're right I'm making this about myself and it's not about me,
though it should be – it's not.
I'm sorry.

MILA
You don't even know what to be sorry for.

MISH
Yes I do!
I told a bad story about some swastikas and blackface.

MILA
You dressed up as a Nazi! You went outside and filmed yourself
dressed up as Nazis with your high school friends. Your childhood
friend was in blackface.

MISH
Prince Harry dressed up as a Nazi and yet everyone loves him.

MILA
I don't love him.

MISH
Plus I was a teenager when that happened. Me and my friends were
stupid then.

MILA
Then why tell the story.

MISH
It was funny.

MISH
No! Not funny. Anymore. In the moment it was but now – Now I get it.

MILA
You don't............ I wrote you a letter.

MILA takes a letter out her bag.

MISH
That's pretty old fashioned. You could have sent an email.

MILA
Sit down.

MISH sits down on the bed.

MILA
It's dark in here.

MISH
You hate light. I turned the lights off because – I can turn them on.

MILA
No. That's great actually...... Okay.

MILA takes in a deep breathe, readying herself.

MILA opens the letter. She begins:

MILA
Michelle,
At first I wasn't angry watching you tell me and others about you and
your friends making a video for class where you dressed up as a Nazi
and your friend danced in blackface. You made it sound like a make-
up tutorial Youtube video. It was a joke and I thought that somehow
there was safety in that. That it was okay because you were laughing.
Slouching in your chair laughing at the memory of your friend's
colored face. You said she used dirt, just peeled it off the ground and
painted it over her face.

Suddenly, I felt sick, dizzy, standing but losing my feet from under me.
But I kept laughing because everyone else was laughing. But when
I left my laughs turned into dark tears, my laugh turned into disgust,
turned into smothered coughs, turned into a need to wash my skin
pure clean. Maybe then she won't tell that story, maybe then she
wouldn't laugh. Maybe then I wouldn't laugh.
Yet even as I stood under a burning shower, hoping to melt my color
off, I wasn't angry at you. I thought you made a mistake. I thought
you I heard you wrong, heard this sick story wrong.
It wasn't until I saw you the next day that I realized I just wanted to
scream at you. I wanted to throw my lungs out at you.
Black lives, Black bodies, Black blood, Black me and you were laughing.

MISH
But –

MILA
I don't know if you understand this but half of my thoughts in my
head are constantly about the color of my skin. Half.
The other half I have to divide up into thinking about school and
family and work and if I get even five percent to think about my
happiness then that's a good day. And yet, half of my thoughts are
about how I'm perceived by others. I don't get to be an individual.
I do one thing wrong and people think oh all black people are like this.
I sit in class and when we talk about some form of race everyone
looks at me including the teacher and what I say they will accept it as
being true for all black people. I don't get to be an individual.
I've never in my life, not since I was five gotten to be an individual.
Most people don't look at me like that. I have to carry the weight of
every single black person on my shoulders.

So when you tell me that your dad's a little racist, that kills me
because now anytime I see him I'm not going to be myself.

MILA
I'll force myself to not speak at all so that I don't say something
that will make him think worse of my whole race.

MISH
My dad wouldn't –

MILA
I'm not saying this to judge your father. His racism is his problem.
Not yours and definitely not mine. I'm telling you this because I
don't know what kind of friends we are. Because you are never
there for me.
You spend most of your time trying to excuse your wrongs and
other people's wrongs than actually dealing with them. You're not
there for me on break-ups or failures. So why would I talk to you
about how being black scares me all the time, that I constantly think
about some cop shooting my brother. You say you don't care about
politics or you don't think it's in your interest to know what's going
on, but to me that directly feels like you're saying you don't care
about me. That you don't give a shit what happens to me or what
I think or how I feel because those issues you never think about
directly effect me, who you vote for effects me more than you
realize because I have a greater chance of dy –
.... I have a greater chance of dying than you. You talk shit about
affirmative action but you never stop to think that without it these
white schools would just admit more white students, not Asian.

And I'm not saying you need to do everything, read everything but
when some big news come out like Eric Garner's killer is going free.
Do you need me to explain to you who that is, I'm not sure you know?

MISH
... I don't.

MILA
He was choked to death by a police officer even though choking
someone is illegal for police officers to do under New York law.

MISH
That seems wrong.

MILA
It is. And it's wrong that I have to explain this shit to you.
I'm not your history teacher, you should know this. You should know
that after learning the officer was going free, I spent all night crying

in my room alone. I don't have that many people here, in this stupid school that I can talk to. You are it for me. You are it for me and I can't even tell you I'm crying because I know you'll just brush it off your shoulders.

And that sucks because I would stop everything for you, everything! If there were ever something that you cared about, that was important to you, I'd learn everything on it. I'd do anything for you, but you wouldn't even look up what racism means in the dictionary.

MISH
I eventually did.

MILA
Then why do I still feel like I've wasted two years trying to be friends with someone who could tell that kind of story in my face and laugh? Why do I have to tell you to pay attention to the world, to care?

And I understand you grew up in an environment that was different than mine and maybe taught you different things than mine. I know you've just been surrounded by other Asians and white people your whole life. But that can't be an excuse for being ignorant. We have the Internet now. You can Google some shit. Or ask me.

And I know, half of this is my fault because I've never talked to you about this and I've been letting this build up and build up for two years now.

MILA
I should have said something sooner because I hate that I haven't talked to you in a week, I hate that you're upset, because all I want is for you to be happy. And whether we stay friends or not, I will still want that for you.

But I can't be the only one who puts in effort into this friendship and who is there when things are bad because it's draining me.

And I can't slice this flesh off of me. I wouldn't want to and you shouldn't want me to. You really shouldn't want me to.

MISH
I don't.

MILA
It feels like you do. Your story felt like you wanted me to hand you my black skin on a silver platter so you can wear it as a joke.

MISH
I – Fuck.

Fuck... Fuck... Fuck! Fuck! Oh – I'm so – Fuck–

272

LETTERS TO A LOST FRIEND

I'm really – I wouldn't want your skin – NOT like that –
I just want you to keep it – it's so – Oh my god –
I'm so sorry – Fuck!
You should have told me this earlier. I wouldn't have –
it wasn't even that funny of story – it was really stupid –
my friend was really stupid – I was – AM really stupid.

My parents don't talk to me about that stuff.
I mean until you, I've only had Asian friends.
You should have told me this earlier.

MILA
You're blaming me for you not doing your own paying attention.

MISH
No. No. I just –
Have I been that bad?

MILA
Yes.

MISH
You were crying?

MILA
All night.

MISH
I… I'm not good with tears.

MILA
I know.

MISH
But I can sit there…uncomfortably with you. I can just sit there.
And I can look up stuff and read up.

MILA
You can protest.

MISH
Protest?

MILA
There's one tomorrow for Eric Garner.

MISH
You don't even protest.

MILA
I didn't realize I was black until coming to this school so yeah,
I protest now.

MISH

That's good. But I can't – I'll help you make signs.

MILA

You can't?

MISH

It's not in me to do things like that. My parents wouldn't approve or anything.

MILA

You're a real model minority aren't you? This idea that you can somehow hide by not being aware of the white bullshit that this world is built on.

MISH

I'm not... I'm not a minority.

Stunned shock.

MILA

Are you kidding me?

MISH

I mean yes, Asians aren't ubiquitous in America but we're not minority status, you know. We're not treated like black people or Muslims or Hispanic people – which is awful and shouldn't happen. I'm not saying it's not awful, it's completely awful and uncalled for but it's just like not applied to us. Asians are a different type of minority.

Let this soak in.

MILA

(Maybe leaning forward a bit.)
Michelle...what do you think is going to happen to you when they get rid of every other color? You think there will be harmony or something between Asians and white America?

MISH

...... Welll – yeah. Sort of. Maybe not harmony but we're basically white. It'll be fine. Post racial – Right?......... Right?

MILA

No.

MISH

.... Oh
.... Oh.

Blackout.

INTIMIDATING
by Allie Woodson

lights up. a young black woman sits on the ground, her legs crossed, her hands in her lap. her hair is up on top of her head, like a crown. she simply sits.

two young black men stand behind her. they watch her. they speak to each other.

jay
ay.
you know her right?

roy
nah. i mean kinda. barely.

jay
bruh, either you do or you don't.

roy
i'm saying like,
i know
of
her.

jay
like you got a class with her or something?

roy
nah. she – you know.

jay
nah – what?

roy
you know.
she like

> *he makes his voice high. "feminine."*

"yeah i just don't party a lot"
"i just don't go out – i got a lot of work"
"i got stuff to do"
"i ain't got time to play"

> *he speaks like himself again.*

you know?

jay
um.
no?

> *roy sucks his teeth.*

roy
bruh. like. uh,

he makes his voice high, again.

"why you always asking for a
hug?" "i'm just minding my
business." "leave me alone."

he speaks like himself again.

on some of that type of stuff.

jay side-eyes roy. hard.

jay
oh.

roy
yeah.
brand new and shit.

silence. they just watch her. then,

jay
bruh, i'm sorry but i'm still confused.
you don't know her
you ain't got a class with her
i'm just –

roy
(annoyed.) nah, bruh, it's like

he makes his voice high, again.

"you following me or something?"
"why every time i'm in here, you in here?"
"no, i don't want to get lunch – i already ate"
"no, i don't want to get dinner – i'm not interested"
"what part of 'leave me alone' don't you understand?"

roy
like – she be trippin man.

jay watches roy, skeptically.

the young woman turns her head in the direction of jay.
she tilts her head; listening.

jay
but i mean,
you ever *actually* talked to her?
like a real conversation? like as friends?

INTIMIDATING

roy
ionno.
like once or twice. she don't hang around with us.

jay
us?

roy
bruh, why you actin real dumb today?

jay
what i'm doin?

roy
just asking a bunch of questions and shit.

jay
since when does asking questions make someone dumb?

roy
i'm just saying like, what's with the 3rd degree and all this shit?

jay
i mean, you act like you know her.

roy
i just know what i hear. i ain't claiming to know her.

> *the young woman laughs. she faces back front.*

jay
well you sure got a lot of opinions for someone who don't know her.

roy
bruh, forreal what do you want from
me? if you wanna know some shit,
shorty sittin right there.

you just go ask her.

jay
why don't you?

roy
'cause you the one with all the questions.

jay
and you the one with all the supposed answers.

roy
you afraid of nothing, bruh.

roy starts forward, confident. the young woman looks upward. she breathes in deeply. she turns her head slightly over her shoulder, waiting.

when she turns he freezes. he scratches his arm. he coughs. he backs up and rejoins jay.

jay
what happened?

roy
nah, bruh
like
she ain't have to look past her shoulder like that like
she ain't even look at me.
who does that?

jay
what?

roy
bruh you saw it.

jay
dude she ain't even do nothin.

roy
that's what i'm sayin like
she ain't like made me feel welcome.

jay
what?

roy
man, i been told you what type of stuff she on.

jay
man, she ain't even do nothin!

roy
that's what im sayin!

jay is confused. roy shrugs him off.

man if that's you, then do
you. ion't fool with her.

roy exits.

jay remains, watching her. he takes a deep breath. he pumps himself up silently. talks himself up. makes himself feel like he can do it. he can talk to her.

INTIMIDATING

he walks up and watches her do the same thing. she looks just past her shoulder, waiting. he gets closer than roy did. even reaches out a hand. he's about to touch her shoulder when he doesn't.

he retreats. in his original spot, he stops. he watches her. she watches just past her shoulder. he sighs. he exits.

she sighs.

she turns to the audience.

she smiles.

dee
she is
i am
too much.

she is
i am
not enough.

she is
i am
alone.

dee
she is i
am
lonely.

she is she is she is

i am i am i am.

    pause.

me.
the one on the side.
the one who hides.
the one who has a lot to
say. doesn't speak her
mind. doesn't have the
time. doesn't shoot her
shot. doesn't want to.

    beat.

well...maybe.
has tried.
still trying.
mind numbing.

brain spinning.
trying to fit in.
trying to stand out.
trying to be everything
to everyone
for everyone
at all times
even when
it feels like
she doesn't want to
doesn't feel like she needs
to feels like she has to
because like solange said
it's **hard**

she sings the line from "F.U.B.U." by solange knowles.

when you're feeling all alone
when you can't even be you up in your home
when you're even getting it from your *own.*

dee
it's hard.
yeah.

and yet.
and yet and yet and yet.

things to do.
places to go.
people to be.
a *person* to be.
a person i *want to be.*
even when it's hard.
and hopefully when it's easier.

can't change.
don't want to.

pause. she thinks. she smiles.

don't think i will.

lights fade.

blackout.

HOOP DREAMS

by Elliot Sagay

TRIP

An ambitious black person who was raised by white parents. Still learning.

ART

An artist who knows so much and so little.

Setting: Trip's office

An office desk. TRIP sits in a nice office chair, is balancing a telephone in one hand and a stress ball in the other.

TRIP

Herbie... Herbie, listen... Why are you listening to Steve? ... I know but, you should – ... No... No, I'm saying I get that his name is on the front sign, but... Herbie, c'mon dude... Seriously? ... Ok, Sir. Better? ... How! How can I be racist? Steve has to listen to the patrons, but aren't they just a bunch of white people anyways? ... But you know me. Brutha – ... Sir. What I don't get is who convinced you that I would be favorin' white people. I mean, have you seen my skin? Anyways, you're the one who calls the shots, are you really gonna let Steve push you around?... Wait, I'm not done talking – ... Herbie, can I call you back, I have a meeting scheduled right now. Should be waiting outside... Oh, yeah. Um. The name's Arthur? Artemus? Ar – ... Yeah! That's the one. Wallace. That's, that's it. He's black. Does that sound like preference to you? ... Covering my ass?

TRIP listens for a while. The ball getting more tense. Then the phone rings.

Hey, Herbie, give me a second, it's Felicia

TRIP presses a button.

Felicia, I told you no calls... Oh... Okay... Really can't wait...
Fine, no, now is good

TRIP presses a different button.

Look, Sir, I need to call you back... No, I don't have a choice – ...
No, I am not "evading the matter at hand" ...

The stress ball loses its effect and TRIP hurls it at the door, just as ART enters. It clocks ART. TRIP stands, or is already standing. Either way TRIP stays behind the desk.

TRIP *(Cont.)*
Shit! Herbie, I will call you back!

TRIP hangs up.

ART
Should I leave, I could –

TRIP
No... No, no, no. Look dude, I'm sorry. I just get a little...passionate at times. Artemus / right?

ART
Actually, Art would be fine...

TRIP *(Continuing without acknowledgement.)*
Well, why don't you come over here. Sit down, relax, recover.
You need anything? I could call Felicia…

ART
I'm good, thanks.

TRIP
Okay, Artemus. Do you know why I called you in here today?

ART
Actually, it's Art.

TRIP
Well, yes, we are in a gallery.

ART
No, I go by Art.

TRIP
Oh…wa-wa-wait. You serious?

TRIP starts laughing.

Art the Artist? Oh shit… What were we talkin' 'bout?

ART
You were gunna tell me why I'm here.

TRIP
Right, right. Gottchyu… So, I looked through this. It's got lots of cool
shit. I'll be straight with ya. I didn't read the poetry, but the art –

Giggles.

TRIP
The art makes up for it. Now, a coupla' other folks have looked and
compiled a list of possible titles for your collection. Listen to this. /
Here we go: –

ART
Um…can I just say

TRIP *(Cont.)*
– Shhh. Don't worry about it. So the first one is, "Lace-less: The
Effects of Poverty in the Hood." Not bad… Not bad at all. Right.
Well, the second is, "Hubris and Hurt: A Juxtaposition of White
Power and Black Subjugation." Clever… I see what they did there.
Then…no…skip that… Oh! "Me" by Artemus Wall – Art Wallace.
Here, you wanna peek? … So, which one's your favorite?

ART pushes TRIP's phone away.

287

ART
Uhhh... I didn't even know you were taking on my project.

TRIP
Well, nothing's official. I'm just getting ahead on my work. Plus, a title would help with pitching your collection to my boss. So, what'd you think?

ART
None of those.

TRIP
Why, you got sumthin' better?

ART
Not yet, but –

TRIP
Well, we wanna take your exhibition to the next level, / so I think –

ART
But I just –

TRIP
– it would be best for you to trust us. Experts / came up with–

ART
I don't care 'bout the –

TRIP
–the titles based on a formula to optimize interest from collectors and our patrons. So, it would be best –

ART
Shut up!

TRIP cautiously sinks into the chair, whispering:

TRIP
Oh.

ART
Sorry.

TRIP
No...no, my bad. The floor is yours.

ART
You don't get it.

TRIP
Get –

ART
The point of my collection, you don't get it. Which is so fucked cuz I bet this gallery had you on this project cuz you are black.

HOOP DREAMS

TRIP
Yeah, that is fucked up... But, what don't I get?

ART
My message, the purpose in these poems and photos and...

TRIP
Actually, I think I do follow. See, I think this thing is making a
statement about how we as the black race live in a prejudiced world
that subjugates our very –

ART
No! This isn't supposed to be another piece about our victimization!
Why do all curators say the same dumb things?

TRIP
Not your first time around the block?

ART
...

TRIP
Well, why don't you tell me what you want the artwork to say?
Beat.

ART
Fine, open this up to a random page with...

ART scans briefly while TRIP flips pages until they come upon...

ART
There, that one.

TRIP
Oh. Yeah, *"Clean."* I remember this photo.

ART
How's it make you feel?

TRIP
Well, it's a little eerie. I mean a skeleton of a bird. I guess maybe
it's commentary about the whiteness of the bone, but then there's
darker tones in the marrow of that broken piece. It could be a
comment on sobriety. Kind of like saying that getting clean can
break you down till you feel like a hollow skeleton? Damn, that is
some deep shit, huh?

ART
There's a story there, ya know? About ten years ago, my dad fried up
a whole chicken from scratch. I just started gettin' into photography
and I had an idea. So I saved all the bones people had left over, and
tried to get a photo of the bird's skeleton.

TRIP
Woah

ART
Yeah. Point is, when I look at that photo, I think of how my ma' wouldn't let me leave the table till I "cleaned the bones." I think about my family gatherin' round the table, and my Grandpa tellin' stories about when he fought in Vietnam, and the smell of sweet potato pie in the oven.

TRIP
But that isn't a message. Is it?

ART
It's the human experience.

TRIP
Really?

ART nods.

TRIP
I don't get it.

Beat.

ART
Thanks for the opportunity.

TRIP
Wait, dude. Let's try again. Okay?

ART
Why?

TRIP
I want to get this. Here, pick another.

ART
Fine, what about this, what do you see here?

TRIP
"Hoop Dreams." Well, it's a shoe. Judging from the back wall, the bullet hole, the untied laces...honestly?

ART nods.

TRIP
I think it's a story? ... A story about how you always wanted to play basketball, but couldn't keep it up because of...gangs and violence.

HOOP DREAMS

ART

But that isn't my shoe. It's my cousin's. And he never joined a gang,
never even got arrested. This photo isn't just memories of playin' ball
or watchin' games. It's so much more. I took the photo with the shoe
so close cuz I figured, it represents how the unfortunate have to step
up and work hard to fill giant shoes, all for a small chance at success.

TRIP

And the basket in the background is the success?

ART

Exactly! Because in this world those opportunities are limited to
a few lucky folks, a few lucky <u>white</u> folk.

TRIP

Wow. Okay… Interesting… So you wanna name it something like
"Hoop Dreams" or "Clean"?

ART

No. It isn't just the naming. I need my work to be marketed as
the telling of an experience.

TRIP

Then what are the take-aways?

ART

That the black experience is a human experience. It's diverse and
messy, but somehow also balanced. Yes, I live life as a victim to
profiling and hate and so much more, but why do people only want
to see me as the person who has been hurt? Nobody wants to
know about all the good times I've had. I am part of one of the most
supportive, loving, communities I could imagine and people still look
at me as if I'm just suffering.

TRIP

But aren't you? I mean, don't you feel scared when a cop looks
your way, doesn't it hurt every time you are reminded of what this
country was, what it still is? Does that really go away?

ART

Maybe it is there, all the time. But isn't it worse where some people
are headed? There are white people who think you and me would
be the same as them if we had white skin. We are getting grouped
under some blanket American identity without acknowledgement of
what makes us different.

TRIP

I think you might be blowing this out of proportion.

A brief stare down.

ART
I have had an incredible amount of people touch my hair without asking, without understanding its history. I once met a German kid who had dread locks because–

ART *(Cont.)*
– he thought they look "cool." But every time something happens to a black person, I become one of many stand ins, so that white people can apologize for what happened without actually addressing the people who lost a family member. What they don't get is that for me, that event is a reminder of how fucked up this society is. But they are apologizing as if I lost my brother or best-friend, when in reality, I didn't know the guy any more than they did. Where's the respect, where is the equal treatment? They say they understand, but time and time again prove their ignorance. And I am tired. Okay?

TRIP
Sure.

ART
I ... I just think it is important for them to see us. To respect us, love us, but also see who we are.

TRIP
Yeah.

ART
Yeah?

TRIP nods.

ART
We good...right?

TRIP
Um.

ART
I don't need to find a new gallery?

TRIP
Oh...no... No, we good, we good.

ART
Cool.

A pause, in thought. ART suppresses a grin of success.

ART
I guess I should get goin'.

TRIP
Right… Hey, lemme know what you wanna call it? … So that we can start marketing for opening.

ART
… Okay, thanks…see ya.

ART leaves. TRIP sits back. Then, opens the portfolio. TRIP reads out loud, but it is ART's voice that is heard.

ART
"Am I racist?
Is it racist to cringe when I see a blank sheet of paper, to laugh when I eat a handful of crackers?
If I don't listen to white rappers by precedent, don't even use the white flavor of Pepsodent,
make my feelings about white privilege evident, am I racist?

I see white teeth underneath two-faced smiles, all the while thinkin' 'bout post-labor day styles,
but the color of the lights that illuminate the aisles in a movie theater bring me to my knees.
Cuz I don't feel safe, never safe, not too safe, can't save myself a spot in the front of a bus. So,

am I racist?
Is my accent racist when I know how to talk white? Am I being racist if I prefer running at night?
See I don't know if I'm racist every time I'm shocked, cuz as I climb through the stages of the day, I make decisions that support stereotypes.

I don't think I'm racist, but I wonder."

TRIP sits back for a long time, considering what was just read. Then, to self:

TRIP
Am I racist…

The phone rings.

TRIP
Herbie, hey man…naw, I actually want to apologize…sure, I get it, warning accepted… But, hey…you gotta promise me, we take on this project…the collection, the one of –

TRIP *(Cont.)*
– photos and poems… I'll have Felicia send you a copy… Oh, um… Artem – I mean, Art, Art Wallace… Trust me Herbie, just trust me on this, it's gonna be great.

MILK

by Amira Danan

AYANA

Has a wish that cannot be granted, admires those who are lucky enough to find shooting stars.

MAMA

A mother before all else. Holds her history behind the whites of her eyes.

Setting: A place you know

Time: A time hungry for change

Note: /– indicates a brief pause

SCENE ONE

AYANA enters, wearing a navy blue dress and a slight frown.
She doesn't wear shoes. She paces around the space, pauses to
inspect the ends of her hair. She looks to the sky. Hums a folk song
she heard on the radio the day before. She stops pacing and sits.

AYANA Why does everyone keep on asking me that? Mama says
it's because they think it's pretty / But I don't think it's pretty.
If they say that, I think they're lying. When Mama brushes it out in
the morning, I scream and scream / but she keeps on pulling. And
even though she pulls her hardest, it never looks right. I try and fix
it once she brings me to the bus stop, but frizz just gets frizzier no
matter what. They always want to touch it / They don't even ask.
Sophie and all the other kids try and pull my curls and I run and
I run and I run / but they keep on coming. And Mama always says
hate is a strong word. But I think I hate it. I don't ask to touch Mary
Ann's hair, even though I want to. Mary Ann is pretty. She has
these golden specks in every strand, and it's not too straight but
not too curly like mine. And when she runs, it bounces in the wind
and it trails right behind her like a wave. And her skin is silky and
smooth and it looks like milk.

I saw a doll in the toy store the other day – it looked just like Mary
Ann. It had these big, big blue eyes like oceans and a fancy pink
dress with frills and white tights. I asked mama if I could buy it and
she said I should wait until my birthday because I have too many
dolls already. I never see any dolls that look like me / Mama says
they're all bought because everyone likes them too much. And
then she looks at me, and she smiles, and she says 'I wish I coulda
gotten you one of those dolls before they sold out'. But I don't think
I want one. I think I'm maybe a little glad they sold out. I wish –
I wish I could cut off all my hair. And I wish it would grow back long
and yellow like a corn field, like Mary Ann's. Don't tell mama
I said that, she'd be angry. Real angry.

SCENE TWO

A rocking chair and a small bowl of colorful beads. AYANA and
MAMA sit together. AYANA on the floor in between her mother's
legs. MAMA on the rocking chair. The chair creaks. She braids
AYANA's hair. AYANA lets out a little whimper every so often.

AYANA Ouch. That hurts.

MILK

MAMA continues braiding.

AYANA I said – OUCH.

MAMA You want me to stop with your head half done?

AYANA No.

MAMA Alright then. Sit still. No more squirming.

AYANA tries to sit still, tries not to squirm.

(Beat.)

Can't sit still. Squirms.

AYANA But it hurts.

MAMA I know, honey, I know. What color beads?

AYANA Purple and then blue and then green and then purple again.

MAMA Good choice.

AYANA A girl I know has flat hair. How does she get it like that?

MAMA She probably uses a hair straightener.

AYANA Can I use one?

MAMA I always liked your braids. We don't want to burn all this beautiful curl away, do we?

AYANA Mary Ann doesn't have hair like mine. She doesn't even have to burn it.

MAMA Mhm. And she doesn't have melanin like yours either, does she?

MAMA kisses AYANA on the cheek, then returns to her work.

AYANA What's that?

MAMA It means your skin is full of sunlight.

AYANA picks up a hand mirror lying on the ground and begins to inspect her braids. Her gaze moves from hair to skin. She touches her face.

AYANA Looks like I rubbed dirt on.

MAMA Now I won't have you talking like that in my house.

AYANA You want me to lie?

MAMA I want you to learn.

AYANA Learn what?

MAMA That dirt is rich. It helps the plants grow. Everything beautiful comes from the earth. You come from the earth, and so do I.

AYANA Fine. Then coal. My skin's black, like coal you get in your stocking if you're bad.

AYANA thinks MAMA isn't looking. She rubs at her arm, to no avail. MAMA leans down and carefully moves AYANA's hand.

MAMA And coal makes diamonds.

AYANA Does not.

MAMA When it has a lot of pressure deep underneath the ground. You are made of diamonds, and rich soil, and all the colors of the rainbow.

AYANA Black isn't in the rainbow, Mama.

MAMA But when you take all those colors together; red, and yellow, blue, and green, orange and indigo / violet / you get us out of it.

MAMA twists strands of AYANA's hair thoughtfully. AYANA is thinking. MAMA begins to hum "Swing Low, Sweet Chariot". AYANA hears her history in the song and looks up with big, brown eyes.

AYANA What's that?

MAMA A song.

AYANA How'd you know it?

MAMA It was given to me.

AYANA Like a present?

MAMA Like a present.

AYANA From who?

MAMA Your ancestors.

AYANA Like grandma? She doesn't like to write songs. She likes to make quilts, she told me last week.

MAMA No, no. Before all of that. Before we had time to make quilts.

AYANA What did they used to be like? Grandma and grandpa but before the quilts.

MAMA They were still grandma and grandpa. But they had a lot less than we have now. There was something missing, something gone that left them feeling empty.

AYANA What did they lose?

MAMA A piece of their liberty.

AYANA How big was the piece?

MAMA Big enough for them to miss it all the time, every second of every day.

AYANA If it was so big, why couldn't they just find it and glue it all back together? You told me to retrace my steps to find something I lost.

MAMA Freedom is real hard to find – hides in places you'd never think to look.

AYANA Oh. Well did they ever get it back?

MAMA In time. But it took them a while to get out of the woods – we sure aren't out yet.

AYANA The woods?

MAMA Mhm.

AYANA How big are the woods?

MAMA Real big. And real wide and thick. And sometimes, you walk through the woods and you look through the trees and you see the sun shine down through the branches and you think you're out. And you run to get to the edge and then you see a shadow and you just can't get around it. And then the sunshine's gone and you're right back in.

AYANA That's sad. That we can't get out of the woods.

MAMA It is sad.

AYANA But, if we keep walking we'll get out of them, won't we?

MAMA You know what? I think you might be right.

AYANA We just keep on walking, and retracing our steps, and we'll find what we lost.

MAMA We just keep on walking.

(Beat.)

MAMA Ms. Clarke called the other day. She said you all did self-portraits in class.

AYANA Yeah, we got to use watercolors, and markers, and –

MAMA She said yours doesn't really look like a self-portrait.

AYANA It does. Just with Mary Ann hair. So I colored with markers and then –

MAMA She said you didn't color on your skin either. Just left it white.

AYANA Yeah.

MAMA Did you forget to color it?

AYANA No. I just added some things. Ms. Clarke never makes any rules. I wanted to draw something good.

MAMA I would've liked to have a drawing of you.

AYANA You can have it, I brought it home today.

MAMA But you didn't really make a self-portrait, did you?

AYANA No

MAMA Maybe you could draw me a brand-new one.

AYANA I don't know if I can.

MAMA I would love to have it.

AYANA I wasn't sure what brown to use.

MAMA What do you mean?

AYANA Well, there's lots of them. Chestnut, Mahogany, Brown, Sepia –

MAMA That does seem like a dilemma.

AYANA Yeah. And I don't know what Sepia is, so I didn't want to use that one –

MAMA Of course

AYANA Yeah. And everyone else was using Peach because they're mostly Peach, so I didn't know what to use because I'm not Peach.

MAMA You ever think about how many choices you have? There's only one kind of Peach.

AYANA I guess

MAMA Mahogany, Chestnut, Sepia, and Brown. You can use every single one – there are so many shades of you.

AYANA I can make my own?

MAMA There are no rules, like you said.

AYANA Mahogany and Chestnut and Sepia *and* Brown –

MAMA You don't even need Peach.

MILK

AYANA's braids don't hurt so much anymore. She stops squirming. She picks up the hand mirror and looks at herself. She sees MAMA in the reflection behind her.

MAMA You're all done.

AYANA Can I start my picture now?

MAMA Let me get you some paper.

MAMA stands to fetch paper and crayons for AYANA. AYANA immediately dumps out the crayons and begins to sift through them, her eyes landing on each shade of herself. She collects them in a small pile and begins to draw. AYANA draws for a while and completes the image with a rainbow above herself.

MAMA That's a lovely rainbow you drew.

AYANA You said that's what I am right?

MAMA Exactly right.

AYANA Can you help me draw a diamond?

MAMA Of course.

AYANA And I want a lot of dirt over here, and I'm going to put a huge flower in it and it's going to be me smelling the flower. And then I hafta leave room over here, for –

AYANA's voice trails off. The look on her face resembles that of a girl who is slowly learning to love four brown crayons.

THREE BLACKBRIDS
by Cat Davidson

SCENE ONE

The stage is black. Nina Simone's "Blackbird" begins to play.

The lights come up on three women standing back to back. ALLIE (22), ANGIE (16), and LONNIE (30).

ALLIE
I'm Allie from Alabama.
And my dad picks cotton on the same land as his great great
grandfather. Yeah that's right his daddy's daddy's daddy was a slave
And now my daddy works for the same last name.
The great great grandson of the slaveowner who whipped his great
grandfather. And now my daddy's scars, they're psychological.
And me…yeah I'm messed up too, you know
Yet everybody keeps telling me slavery was a long time ago.

The circle of women turn.

ANGIE
I'm Angie. And here I am sitting in History
And my teacher starts talking about
slavery and everyone turns to look at me.
And they're all like "What was it like?"
Fuck I know. My great grandparents were free black folks. Besides
does it look like I'm back in 1835
Eating chitlins and getting cutting eyes from the slave masser's wife?
Why don't you tell me? Read a book. Like Frederick Douglass.
Let him tell you how it was and how much he couldn't stomach it.
Then my teacher turns to the poster of Frederick Douglass on her
wall
And says she doesn't understand why anyone wouldn't take him
seriously "He looks more Native American than Black to me."
What the fuck is that?
Does it matter whether he looks more or less black?
And excuse me Native Americans are treated just as badly. Sadly.
But I guess, according to her, the more African he looks the less
intelligent he would be. Seriously? Seriously.

The circle of women turn.

LONNIE
My name is Lonnie and I respect Rachel Dolezal!
You know, for trying to get by as a Black Female!
If she felt like the only way she could accomplish what she wanted
to do was to impersonate a black woman: Well why the hell not?

How is that any different from the thousands of black people out there who could "pass" for white. They did what they felt like they had to do to accomplish their goals.

And yeah, yeah, yeah… I know. There's a whole lot more to it than that: like self-denial and the hypocrisy of the "one drop rule". But geez. Why all the beef?

This was probably the first time in history that somebody wanted to "pass for black"! So I say: More power to that!

ANGIE
More power to that!

ALLIE
More power to:

LONNIE
Deciding to be a doctor AND a poet.

ALLIE
To being a leader not a follower.

ANGIE
To wearing my natural hair.

ALLIE
To smiling when there seems like nothing to smile about.

ANGIE
More power to believing in something greater than myself.

LONNIE
More power to believing in myself.

ALLIE
More power to my power. To your power.

ANGIE
More power to reaching back.

LONNIE
And pulling another one forward.

ALLIE
To holding hands with friends.

They all hold hands.

ANGIE
To opening a door for a stranger.

LONNIE
To finding peace.

THREE BLACKBIRDS

ALLIE
Reaching for dreams.

ANGIE
More power to love. To loving myself.

LONNIE and ALLIE
To loving my power!

ALL
To loving me.

The three break away from each other. LONNIE steps forward.
ANGIE and ALLIE remain on stage. Sometimes they move in short
lyrical movements when they are overcome with emotion.

LONNIE
Use to think I was unlovable. My skin was too untouchable.
"Wouldn't want to kiss her." "You're cute for a black girl." "I love my
grandma, and she wouldn't like you." Took years to stop giving away
myself to every jackass that looked in my direction. Giving away a
little piece of myself that they would throw away. Discard like trash
in an incinerator. Taking years to get those ashes back. Wrote a love
poem to myself. Wanna hear it?: Goodbye princess in your ivory
tower.
Didn't you know your stones are made of coal.
Burning black embers flame and cinder under foot and you are left
standing in a pile of your own dirt.
Runaway little princess to the inner-most cave. The dark shadows full
of loneliness,
Wet dripping tears coming through the cracks in the walls.
Cool earth seducing you. Saying return to me.
But one ember still flares bright in your hair and sets you a flame.
You princess are glowing. Glowing, bright red, shining deep brown,
bright yellows, and all the while you had thought you were just a
princess. Turns out, you're a goddess!

ANGIE joins LONNIE.

ANGIE
Goddess. Blackness.

LONNIE
What does it mean?

ANGIE
Originality, Swag.

LONNIE
Dance, Music, Art!

ANGIE
Everyone tries to duplicate it.

LONNIE
Can't be taught!

ANGIE and LONNIE do their secret hand shake that leads into a step! ALLIE joins the step!

ALLIE
Do you like the color of your skin?

LONNIE
Yes.

ALLIE
What is it?

LONNIE
Chocolate. With a little vanilla.

ANGIE
You know vanilla's black right?

The women stop stepping. LONNIE and ALLIE exchange a look.

ANGIE
Comes from an orchid. Raw vanilla are these black little seeds.

LONNIE
Is the Orchid white?

ALLIE
It's a vagina!

LONNIE
What!

ALLIE
Orchids look like vaginas.

ANGIE
True.

LONNIE
So vanilla comes from a vagina?

ANGIE
Yeah!

LONNIE
And vanilla is black?

THREE BLACKBIRDS

ALLIE
Hahaha!

ANGIE
Yeah!

ALLIE
Imagine that.

LONNIE
So does chocolate come from a vagina too?

ALLIE
Chocolate comes from an ovary.

LONNIE
Excuse me?

ALLIE
The ovary of a cocoa tree is a cocoa pod which houses the seeds.
Chocolate is made from the " cocoa beans", which are like chocolate eggs!

LONNIE
This is way too biological for me.

ALLIE
It's all biological.

LONNIE
I'm never going to think of a ho-ho in the same way.

ANGIE
Now that's just artificial flavoring.

LONNIE throws her hands up and walks away.

ALLIE
Lonnie, wait! Did I tell you coffee is mother earth's milk!

LONNIE
Now you're just making things up.
Angie whips around.

ANGIE
Did I tell about the time I went home and told my dad this white guy
had just asked me out! And my dad said "No".

ALLIE
No?

ANGIE
Yeah, no! I had just won Miss Black Teen Connecticut and my dad
said I was representing my race. "You don't need to be seen out

with some white boy gallivanting around town." I said "It's just a date. Ain't like I'm going to marry him." My dad said Miss Black Teen Connecticut is more than just a beauty pageant and I better understand what it meant. Then he said to me. Go ask him if he told his parents you're black.

LONNIE
Ohhhh.

ALLIE
Did he?

ANGIE
So the next day I marched up to him and asked. "Did you tell your parents I was black?" He said "no". And that was that!

ALLIE
Oh.

ANGIE
Didn't stop me from dating white guys once I was done being Miss Teen Connecticut!

LONNIE
I know that's right. I date all kinds of guys. Big guys, tall guys.

ALLIE
What about short guys, small guys?

LONNIE
Uh? No.

They laugh.

ALLIE
Give me a Puerto Rican brother with some Afro-latino swagger.

LONNIE
I'm sold.

ANGIE
Me too! Give me a Bruce Lee, a Marc Anthony, and a Terrence Howard.

LONNIE
A Terrance Howard?

ALLIE
Oh no he's too creepy for me.

LONNIE
It's the eyes.

ANGIE
Now see there you two go judging a man for his beautiful eyes.

LONNIE
He always be playing those sketchy characters.

ANGIE
That doesn't mean the man's sketch. Judge not lest ye wants to be judged.

LONNIE
Judging is in our DNA. "And the humans came and judged the whole world and the world was swallowed up by hate cause they didn't like what they saw. And they looked at their work and saw that it was bad. But the final hour had come and it was too late to turn back."

ALLIE
What verse is that?

ANGIE
Executive Order 666.

LONNIE
I'm straight up stressing right now.

ANGIE
Use to it.

ALLIE
Feel it more now!

ANGIE
Really?

ALLIE
The closeness of the hate.

LONNIE
Seems the same.

ALLIE
You know what's changed?

ANGIE
Nothing?

ALLIE
Nina reads me like a book. Sings into my soul. "I'm just a soul who's intentions are good. Oh Lord, please don't let me be misunderstood." *(Beat.)* I already knew. Knew it was going to happen. But what does that matter. Knowing don't mean nothing.

Don't mean nothin without action. If tomorrow I told you you were gonna die. What would you do? You'd tell me I was crazy. But it's true. Tomorrow someone out there in the world is going to die. And I'm using the universal you. If I can use the universal "You", then why can't you see me universally. Why is it "you and me"? You and me. Why can't it be "we" indefinitely? I think about the City of the Blind. You know that story where the "one-eyed man is king". You know I feel sorry for the king. Cause he's the only one judging. And I bet you he closes his eye sometimes, just to be like everybody else. Just to feel the way everyone else does. There must be safety in that. But then I bet you he opens his eye again. Doesn't want to keep it shut and miss out on the beauty of it all.

LONNIE and ANGIE stare at ALLIE. LONNIE starts to sing.

LONNIE
Why you wanna fly blackbird?

ANGIE
You ain't ever gonna fly.

LONNIE
Why you wanna fly blackbird?

ANGIE
You ain't every gonna fly.

LONNIE
Why you wanna–

ALLIE
Fly Blackbird!

LONNIE
But I'm scared to fly. As soon as I get off of the plane, feel eyes judging me. Feel hands pushing me. Feel my heart racing. Feel words spit at me from brains trained to look at me differently. Feel trapped. Clastrophobic. Not free. Feel the fear of my fellow refugee. Fly blackbird, fly.

ANGIE
Gotta fly cause they said I can't.

ALLIE
Gotta fly cause God gave me wings.

ANGIE
And a brain to invent things.

LONNIE
Hands to heal.

THREE BLACKBIRDS

ALLIE
A voice to share.

LONNIE
A story to tell.

ALL
A life to live.

The three come together for one final dance to Nina Simone's "Feeling Good".

The End.

JUST A THOUGHT

by Chloe Noelle Fourte

A'ISHA sits on the edge of a rooftop. She is smoking a cigarette, and is at ease.

She's not happy, but she's not sad.

It is night. The wind is whistling at her back. Any other person would be scared they would fall with the wind, but she is not.

A single spotlight.

A'ISHA
(She addresses the audience as if speaking to a long-lost friend with whom she desperately seeks to reconnect.)

No. I'm not gonna jump. I'm not stupid. I'm not even that sad. I mean, I'm sad, but not that sad. I mean I don't think I am... Well, I'm not gonna jump, so don't worry about me. I could never actually do it. Besides I'm pretty sure this is the only request my parents had for me when I came to college: please, just don't kill yourself. Ha. "Please. Don't kill yourself." As if suicide is like getting drunk or becoming a stoner. Yes, mama, I'll try.

Ironically, they named me life. Well, not literally. The name they gave me means life. A'isha. I-EE-SHUH. Spelled, A-apostrophe-I-S-H-A. A'isha Glendale Clarke. Ha! Man you should see y'all's faces. You guys lookin at me like, 'Girl please. That ghetto name don't mean shit. Yo mama made it up. Stop lyin.' But deadass man. It means life. That's actually why they chose it. I think they thought it would work like protection, kind of like a prophecy or something. Like it might absolve me of my family's inheritance of death. A plea of hope into the empty void, if you will. Ha. We'll see how it works.

Actually, A'isha is Arabic. Ya, for real. A'isha was the name of the favorite wife of Prophet Muhammad. She was hella smart. That's pretty much all I know.

I was raised Christian, so I don't really know much about the history or why they named me A'isha. I honestly think I could've done good with a basic Bible name like Sarah or Rachel, or even gone full Anglo with something like Elizabeth or Lilian. It was just so awkward going to a school full of Victorias and Jessicas with a name like A'isha. Man, and people would get really confused when they found out I had two married parents and wasn't born in a crackhouse. As if my name was a confirmation for everything they saw wrong with the color of my skin. Well, you thought wrong, bitch. Try again.

I loved that school too, is the fucked up thing. Like I craved the negative attention. You just get so used to being the other that it becomes like some kind of reaffirmation of your importance. Ha.

313

Man don't look at me like that. You woulda fell into the same shit. Same as me.

My parents really got me fucked up though. Like how the hell am I supposed to get a job with the name A'isha? Ha. Man even if I do manage to not kill myself, I might still die from hunger when I don't get a job.

Beat.

I'm not gonna lie, I've thought about the jump before. I'm not gonna do it, but I have thought about it.

BASS. TRUMPET. VOICE.

by Kori Alston

1. BASS

2. TRUMPET

3. VOICE

Note: This is a jam session.

Three black musicians, Bass, Trumpet, and Voice, enter an empty stage.

At first, they do not really acknowledge each other.

Bass mimes tuning an upright bass, vocally imitating his instrument.

Trumpet mimes testing out their trumpet, vocally imitating their instrument. Voice does a few vocal warmups.

In silence, they acknowledge the audience.

After a moment, they turn to each other:

BASS. TRUMPET. VOICE.

1. Ready?

2. Ready.

3. Ready.

1. Five, six, five, six, seven, eight.

2. This song is for the heavens.

1. For the soil. For the earth.

2. This song is for our ancestors.

1. For roots, centuries deep.

2. This song is for acacia trees.

1. For womanhood. For melanin.

2. This is ain't a melody for the wealthy.

1. Not for the rich – the content.

2. Not for the piggybank boys and girls.　　**3.** Oh those piggybank boys and girls,

1. Cash fat. Stock slop.　　　　　　　　　　Cash fat, stock slop.

2. Spinning, spinning, losing, stealing　　　Dizzy, dizzy, lost thieves.

1. Trust funds, white white.　　　　　　　　Trusted, white white.

2. Stealing from you and me and me　　　Robbin' and mobbin' – and you

1. Everyday, from you and me.　　　　　　Everyday, from you and me

2. Can't I get a piece a pie, please?

1. No pie. No pie for you.　　　　　　　　　No pie. No pie for you.

2. Can't I get a hit of that green, please?

1. No green. No green for you.　　　　　　**3.** No green. No green
　　　　　　　　　　　　　　　　　　　　　　for you

2. Please, brother man – I'm beggin' ya!

1. No, none for the spades.

2. None for the brothers and sisters here?

1. No, none for the spades.

2. But we playin' for you, brother man!

1. Sorry, Sambo.

2. Oh, no, no, no, no, no!

1. Sorry, Jim Crow.

2. Hell no, no, no, no, no!

1. Come down, brother please.

2. But I'm tryna get high, brother man!

1. Brother, please.　　　　　　　　　　　**3.** I'm tryna get high, so high

2. Brother, please!　　　　　　　　　　　　　　– Up past the city systems

1. Brother, please.　　　　　　　　　　　　　Past the telephone sisters

2. Brother, please!　　　　　　　　　　　　　And pigs, and piggybanks

1. Brother, please.　　　　　　　　　　　　　– All the way up, so high –

2. Brother, please!　　　　　　　　　　　　　I want solar systems

1. Brother, please.　　　　　　　　　　　　　And Afro-Future Soul Sisters

2. Brother, please!　　　　　　　　　　　　　Higher than the freedom

1. Brother, please.　　　　　　　　　　　　　tower – I said,

2. Brother, please!　　　　　　　　　　　　　"Brother, please, brother,
　　　　　　　　　　　　　　　　　　　　　　　please!"

1. Brother, please.　　　　　　　　　　　　　But pigs got 'em caged
　　　　　　　　　　　　　　　　　　　　　　　quick –

2. Brother, please!　　　　　　　　　　　　　I poured out my pockets

1. Brother, please.　　　　　　　　　　　　　Put the pennies on
　　　　　　　　　　　　　　　　　　　　　　　the table

2. Brother, please!　　　　　　　　　　　　　Thought maybe it would
　　　　　　　　　　　　　　　　　　　　　　　make me lighter

BASS. TRUMPET. VOICE.

1. Brother, please.

Make me fly higher,
shine brighter –

2. Brother, please!

But I'm still on the
ground, in my Air Ones

1. Brother, please.

Sayin',

2. Brother, please!

1. Brother, please. Brother, please!

2. On vocals, Amira Danan

2. Brother, please!

1. Brother, please.

2. Brother, please!

1. Brother, please.

3. Tell 'em, brother bass!

Pick up, brush off,

Afro, full lips

Skin rich, eyes deep

Dig deep, find peace

Breathe, breathe, break free

Set goals, get clean

Smoke loud, smoke green

Love you, self esteem

Stay true, find the key

Find the cage, set them free

River Jordan,

carry me Wade
to freedom,

Set me free,

Brother please,
you're killing me

Brother please,

Set me free

Brother please, you're
killing me

Brother, please,
brother, please

Brother, please

Set me free

Brother, please

Set me free

Brother, please

1. Set me free

Brother, please

Set me free

Brother, please

Set me free

Brother, please

Set me free

Brother, please

Set me free

Brother, please

Set me free

Brother, please

Set me free

Brother, please

Set me free

Brother, please

Set me free

Brother, please

Set me free

Brother, please

Set me free

Brother, please

Set me free

BASS. TRUMPET. VOICE.

3. Ryan Foreman on the bass!

2. Melodies from mother

Country-hunted

Can't hide our hides

2. Can't seem to break 'em free   **3.** Set me free

From the trees

And penitentiaries   **3.** Set me free

Centuries on centuries

Of killing us so senselessly   **3.** Set me free

Since Malcom

Since Nat T   **3.** Set me free

Since Kinte

Since Mum B   **3.** Set me free

Since the colonies in the Congo

The greatest import of the west   **3.** Set me free

We still runnin' from the slave catchers

Runnin', runnin' from the house masters   **3.** Set me free

Still runnin' like its Sunday

In our Sunday's best –   **3.** Set me free

Worn on Tuesdays too

Wednesdays, Thursdays   **3.** Set me free

You never know when the bullet's ready

When their fingers are particularly fidgety   **3.** Set me free

Sniffin' for ya

Itchin' for ya   **3.** Set me free

Their addicted to ya

Your hips, your kicks   **3.** Set me free

Brother, please

Set me free

Brother, please

Set me free

Brother, please

Set me free

1. Brother, please

Set me free

Brother, please

Set me free

Brother, please

Set me free

Brother, please

Set me free

Brother, please

Set me free

Brother, please

Set me free

Brother, please

Set me free

Brother, please

Set me free

Brother, please

Set me free

Brother, please

Set me free

Brother, please

Set me free

Brother, please

BASS. TRUMPET. VOICE.

Your beats, your flicks

Your hops, your hips

3. Set me free

Your brothers, your sisters

Your aunties, your cousins

3. Set me free

They want your heart,

They want your soul,

3. Set me free

So hold on –

3. Robert Cunningham
on trumpet!

2. Hold on –

2. So Hold on –

3. We sing our songs for:

Alton Sterling and

Michael Brown and

2. Hold on –

Sandra Bland and

Eric Garner and

Kimani Gray and

Nizah Morris and

2. So hold on –

Emmett Till and

Tamir Rice and

Freddie Gray and

Dontre Hamilton and

2. Hold on –

John Crawford and

Ezell Ford and

Dante Parker and

KORI ALSTON

Set me free

Brother, please

Set me free

Brother, please

Set me free

Brother, please

1. Set me free

Brother, please

Set me free

Brother, please

Set me free

Brother, please

Set me free

3. *Oh yes we will.*

BASS. TRUMPET. VOICE.

	Tanisha Anderson and
2. So hold on –	Akai Gurley and
	Rumain Brisbon and
	Jerame Reid and
	Tony Robinson and
2. Hold on –	Phillip White and
	3. Eric Harris and
	Walter Scott and
	Laquan McDonald
2. So hold on –	So hold on –
Hold on	Dig deep
Keep holdin' on!	Fight hard
Hold on –	Hold on –
	1, 2, 3. 'Cause someday
	We'll be
	Set free.

What is Black Lives, Black Words International Project?

Black Lives, Black Words aims to explore the black diaspora experiences in some of the largest multicultural cities in the world, Chicago, Minneapolis, Charlotte, Baltimore, DC, London, UK and more to investigate the question 'Do black lives matter today?'. This project will serve as a comparative study to raise awareness of the shared and different transatlantic experiences in the black community and evaluate the impact it has had on the black community at large.

Black Lives Black Words gathers visual artists, spoken word poets, and between six to nine local black playwrights and have them write ten minute plays based upon the theme "Do Black Lives Matter?".

This project has taken place already in Chicago, produced by Congo Square, MPAACT, ETA Creative Arts, Black Ensemble Theatre's Black Playwright Initiative, and Pegasus Theatre on July 28th, 2015 at the Greenhouse Theatre, then in London, England produced by the Artistic Directors of the Future (an initiative dedicated to increase the amount of Black, Asian and Minority Ethnic (BAME) Artistic Directors in mainstream producing theatres) and the Bush Theatre with the support of WAC Arts and Theatre Royal Stratford East on Oct. 27th. This was followed by Minneapolis at the Guthrie Theatre with Carlyle Brown and Company, Bedlam Theatre, Freestyle Theatre, and the Million Artist Movement on Jan. 19th, 2016 and returned to London, England March 16th, 2016 at the Bush Theatre, produced by the Artistic Directors of the Future. After that we had a second return to Chicago with the project featuring an exciting group of writers and has pushed into Toronto which was produced by Buddies and Bad Times Theatre, Obsidian Theatre, and the National Arts Centre, along with several satellite installations in various cities showcasing the works of these artists. This brings the number of writers we've showcased to over sixty, and the number of diverse actors we've placed on stage almost two hundred strong. We're expanding our vision now, creating what we call College Takeovers providing students the opportunity to produce their own version of Black Lives, Black Words. We've introduced our first College Takeover at Northwestern University in Evanston, IL which is student produced led by BLBW Associate Artist Aaron Todd Douglas and playwright Laura Schellhardt. It's been an exciting journey and we have a long way to go in our mission to speak for the unheard voices.

Managing Curating Producer
Reginald Edmund

Executive Producer
Simeilia Hodge-Dallaway

Senior Coordinating Producer – UK
Simeilia Hodge-Dallaway

Senior Coordinating Producer – Canada
Mel Hague

Senior Coordinating Producers – US
Kyle Haden

Black Lives, Black Words – Artistic Associates
Courttia Newland (London), Wardell Julius Clark (Chicago), Idris Goodwin (Denver), LeeLee Davis (Toronto), Andre Richardson Hogan II (Chicago), Shariba Rivers (Chicago), Aaron Todd Douglas (Chicago), Becca Browne (Chicago), Elana Elyce (Chicago), Daryl Brooks (Chicago), Eric Walker (Houston), Destiny Strothers (Chicago), Charlita Williams (Chicago), Jeff Kirkman III (Washington, DC), Quintin Talley (Charlotte), Ana Velazquez (Chicago), Rachel DuBose (Chicago), Osiris Khepera (Chicago), Loy Webb (Chicago), Dominique Morisseau (Brooklyn, Los Angeles, Detroit), Guadalís Del Carmen (New York), Nicole Michelle Haskins (Detroit, Chicago), Kevin N. Holt (Chicago), Angela Alise (Chicago), Ilesa Duncan (Chicago), Luke Reece (Toronto), Marsha Estell (Chicago), Harrison David Rivers (Saint Paul), Wendy 'Motion' Brathwaite (Toronto), Toma Langston (Chicago), Aaron C. Holland (Chicago), Tiffany Nichole Greene (Houston/Dallas), Kyle Haden (Pittsburgh), Mel Hague (Toronto), Ashley Honore Roberson(Chicago), Hana L. Anderson (Chicago)